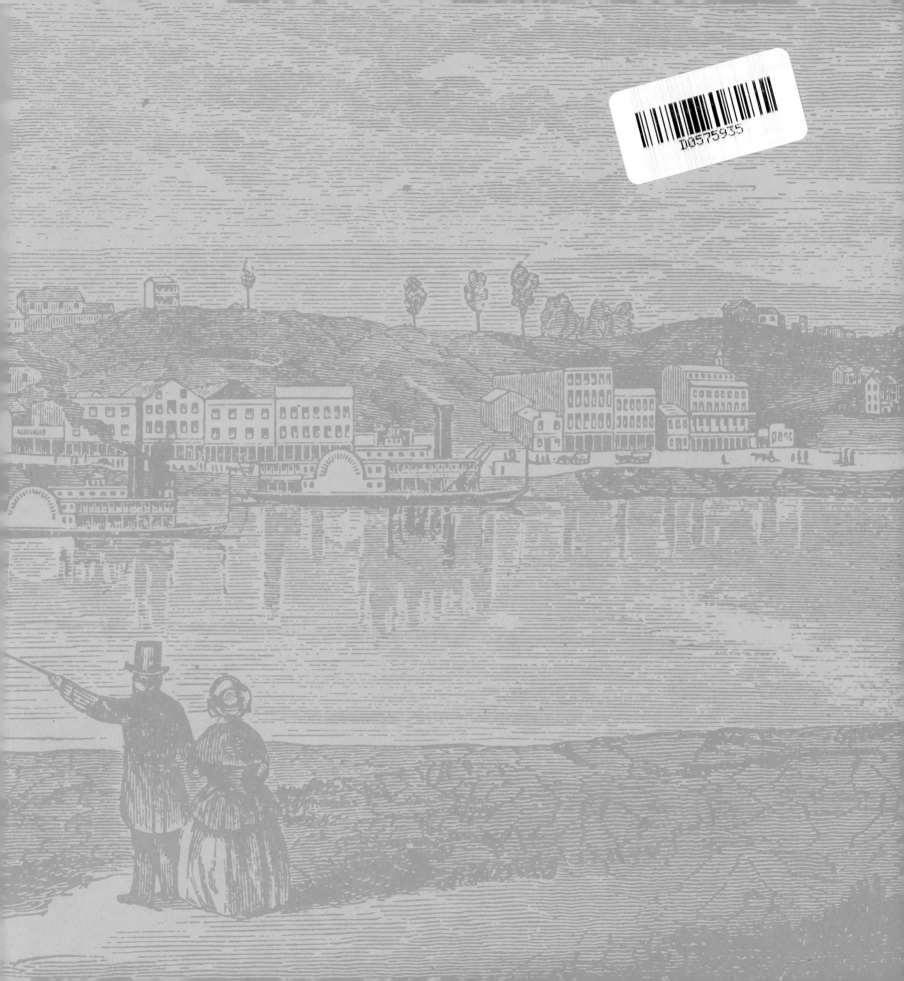

Kansas City

Kansas City

An Intimate Portrait
of the Surprising City on the Missouri

*High atop Kansas City's Penn Valley Park,
Cyrus E. Dallin's award winning statue,
"The Scout," looks from the past to the
future. The monument was built to honor
the Indian plainsman of the American
frontier. It was first shown at the
San Francisco Exposition, then brought to
Kansas City where it found a permanent
home in 1922. Kansas Citians so loved
Dallin's work that they launched a
special subscription drive to purchase
the sculpture for the city.*

Hallmark Cards, Inc. Kansas City, Missouri

ACKNOWLEDGMENTS: Excerpt from "The Ozarks" by Thomas Hart Benton in *Travel & Leisure*. Copyright © 1979 American Express Publishing Corporation. Reprinted by permission. Excerpt from *Ladies' Home Journal* (February 1921). © 1921 Downe Publishing Inc. Reprinted by permission of *Ladies' Home Journal*. Excerpt from *The People, Yes* by Carl Sandburg, copyright, 1936, by Harcourt Brace Jovanovich, Inc., copyright 1964, by Carl Sandburg. Reprinted by permission of the publisher. Excerpts by Debs Myers and the excerpt from "Return to Kansas City" by Edward Dahlberg taken from *Holiday* magazine, now published by Travel Magazine Inc., Floral Park, New York 11001. Reprinted with permission. Excerpts from *CITY OF THE FUTURE, A Narrative History of Kansas City, 1850-1950*, by Henry C. Haskell, Jr., and Richard B. Fowler. Copyright 1950 by the Kansas City Star Company and Frank Glenn Publishing Company. Reprinted by arrangement with the Kansas City Star Company. Excerpt from *Wyatt Earp, Frontier Marshal* by Stuart N. Lake. Copyright 1931. Reprinted by permission of Carolyn Lake. Excerpt by Calvin Trillin. Copyright © 1972 by Calvin Trillin. Reprinted by permission of Robert Lescher. Excerpt from the book *From My Journal* by Andre Maurois. Copyright, 1947, 1948 by Andre Maurois. Reprinted by permission of Gerald Maurois. Excerpt from "Who Jesse Clyde Nichols Is" by John F. Sinclair in *Waterbury American* (April 7, 1928 issue). Copyright, 1928, by North American Newspaper Alliance. Reprinted by permission of North American Newspaper Alliance. Excerpts from *CROSSROADS OF AMERICA, The Story of Kansas City*, by Darrell Garwood, with the permission of W. W. Norton & Company, Inc. Copyright 1948 by W. W. Norton & Company, Inc. Copyright renewed 1976. Excerpt from "Updating Kansas City" by Herbert Silverman in *Travel & Leisure*. Copyright © 1979 American Express Publishing Corporation. Reprinted by permission of the author and *Travel & Leisure*. Excerpts reprinted from *Frontier Community: Kansas City to 1870* by A. Theodore Brown, by permission of the University of Missouri Press. Copyright 1963 by The Curators of the University of Missouri. Excerpt from "Kansas City: Gateway to What?" by W. G. Clugston from *Our Fair City*, Ed. Robert S. Allen. Copyright 1947; Copyright renewed © 1974 by Robert S. Allen. Reprinted by permission of the publisher, the Vanguard Press, Inc. Excerpt from *The New York Times* © 1976 by The New York Times Company. Reprinted by permission. Excerpt from the *Milwaukee Journal* reprinted by permission. Excerpt from *The Washington Post* © The Washington Post. Reprinted by permission. Excerpt by Howard K. Smith Commentary from the ABC Evening News, August 12, 1976.

Contents

Foreword

When the first edition of this book was introduced, we anticipated certain questions: Why a book about Kansas City? Especially, why such a grand book without axes to grind or special interests to serve? Why a book more in tune with Mr. Everyman than with Mr. Business?

We realized our book on our Kansas City was taking a position among the great city books of Europe, following a pattern set by splendid examples found in Paris, London, Copenhagen, and Munich. At that time, in 1972, it was agreed that Kansas City was "one of America's best kept secrets." We wanted to change that, in our own way.

The success of that first edition substantiated the dreams of the young creative team within Hallmark that controlled that edition as they do this new, second edition. The photographers, writers, and designers who have compiled both editions are determined that their creation not carry any self-serving purpose. It is their book about their city. If it happens to serve economic development interests, fine, but its intent is not to sell real estate. If it happens to boost tourism and lure new business, splendid, but its charter was not from the Chamber of Commerce. Its sole purpose is to inform more people about the visual pleasures, history, and current activities of a wonderful metropolitan area — a community — we call home. As befits a book created by talented Kansas Citians, they insisted that the production of this book reflect the work of local Kansas City craftsmen, including all color separation, printing and lithography.

The second edition is a mandate from the purchasers of the first edition. As three printings were steadily sold out, it was decided not to reprint again until the book could be properly updated. This community is changing too rapidly, progressing too quickly to allow 1973 photographs to represent its contemporary portrait. In the past few years, both Bartle Convention Center and the Kemper Arena have been constructed, the latter hosting the 1976 GOP National Convention. The downtown skyline has added several impressive new buildings by architects such as Harry Weese and Gyo Obata. Progress has continued at Crown Center and the Country Club Plaza. Marvelous additions and acquisitions have come to the Nelson Gallery, the park system, the Philharmonic, and our colleges and universities. The Performing Arts Center is open and flourishing.

Such physical progress has commanded this new edition. But those of us who live here also note continued improvements in our quality of life and the fun and friendship we enjoy when together. Our city has long been a pleasant home, a place of wooded hills, ample water, and gracious people. We have completed a decade of remarkable progress, buoyed by both optimism and construction and fueled by aroused civic energies and well-earned civic pride.

This edition, then, is offered to the people of Kansas City, their friends, and our visitors. In words and pictures it documents our place, Kansas City, the surprising city on the Missouri.

— Donald J. Hall, President, Hallmark Cards, Inc.

This Place, This Kansas City

If you were told that at one time or another Kansas City has been compared to Paris, Seville, and Istanbul, would you believe it? It is, of course, none of these — and yet such comparisons, and others, have been made by persons of considerable taste and discernment. Whether upon reflection you can agree or not, certainly this place, this Kansas City, can hardly be described in terms of a typical prairie environment.

It is, without argument, a city full of surprises. Consider that Kansas City is built on more hills than ancient Rome. And that it is, believe it or not, grassier than Ireland. Who but the initiated would expect Kansas City to abound with water? It is known as a city of fountains; and as well as the mighty Missouri that flows along its northern border, the area is graced with a myriad of ponds and lakes.

It is a city of parks — 125 of them. As native Kansas Citian Edward Dahlberg once observed, "One can go almost anywhere and be eased by the blossoms of the magnolias in the spring, or fall into a soft, moody melancholia when autumn has unclothed the oak, maple, cherry, and forsythia."

No less an authority than Andre Maurois, one of the toughest French intellectuals of the twentieth century, places Kansas City among the world's most beautiful cities. Maurois spent several months in the area during World War II and later wrote in From My Journal: "Who in Europe, or in America for that matter, knows that Kansas City is one of the loveliest cities on earth?"

A city in the middle of the plains that inspires such descriptive praise indeed may not be a Paris or a Rome; it need not be, for its own personality must emerge, and in time other cities will be compared to it. Kansas City has emerged — a place to be reckoned with, a place that has become what people say it is: "a new kind of city."

The city is complex — a collage of fifty towns in two states and six counties, dissected by meandering rivers and creeks, interrupted by hills and woodlands. Each municipality is fiercely chauvinistic. Kansas City, Kansas, touts its grain elevators and rail centers. Independence is "Harry's town." The wealthy suburb of Mission Hills is justifiably proud of its elegance and style. Small community loyalties make Kansas City a pleasant, easy place in which to live. But let the Royals get to the league play-offs or the Republicans come to town, and Raytown or Shawnee citizens become urbanites — participants and believers in the idea of Greater Kansas City.

Kansas City grew first upon the bluffs overlooking the river. The northwest corner of downtown is named Clark's Point (for Councilman Charlie Clark, a crony of Tom Pendergast), although it is better known as Lewis and Clark Point. In 1806 the two explorers returned from the Pacific and scaled this spot. Here their men shot elk and gathered custard apples, or pawpaws. They wrote in their journal that the bluff was ideal for a fort and "from the top of the hill you have a perfect command of the river." But the full brunt of this bluff is best felt below, from the Lewis and Clark Viaduct, connecting Kansas City, Kansas, with Kansas City, Missouri.

Traveling east, you look up at the skyline perched atop a massive limestone outcrop. It is not the Matterhorn, but it must have surprised settlers as it surprises people today.

Whatever "downtown" once meant to Americans, it meant to Kansas Citians. Everything important was there: back-to-school clothes, Fourth of July speeches, talking movies, all official business, and the Sodoms and Gomorrahs of sin. Downtown was uptown — expensive and exciting. Post-World War II lifestyles changed Kansas City's downtown as it did downtowns everywhere. What was once uptown lost out to greener, more spacious suburbia.

But fortunately, in the early 1960s, a cluster of civic-minded local business leaders with a sense of pragmatism and timing created a downtown master plan. The dormant city was awakening.

Few vestiges of the halcyon years remain, yet landmark buildings are protected by those who treasure the past. The Folly Theater, where the likes of Sarah Bernhardt and Al Jolson performed, is being saved from demolition and will be restored to grandeur. Yet the emphasis downtown these days is on the new. The urban renaissance is on. City Center Square rises thirty stories high and fills a city block. White, angular, it assertively alters the city skyline. The brown steel and glass Mercantile Bank and Trust seems to perch precariously on a slender pillar. Next to the blue-mirrored Executive Plaza, the new Merchant's Bank, in camel-hued concrete, hugs the Main Street pavement.

Beyond the venerable Radisson Muehlebach Hotel, the H. Roe Bartle Exposition Hall lays claim to the western horizon. Its gray walls, a series of horizontal structural steel triangles, enclose a four-and-a-half-acre unpillared space. With a ceiling forty feet high and room for 20,000 chairs, the Bartle has hosted everything from

"I hear America singing, the varied carols I hear:
Those of mechanics – each one singing his as it should be, blithe and strong;
The carpenter singing his, as he measures his plank or beam,
The mason singing his, as he makes ready for work, or leaves off work...."
  Walt Whitman

Here in downtown is where the song is sung with feeling, a song of progress and rebirth, accelerating in interest and confidence with the pounding of jackhammers and the bass rumble of backhoes and bulldozers. Here men make music in concrete and steel. Here architects' daring dreams alter the urban skyline with the thrust of new geometrics. Here generations of dreams wrought in brick and wood are reflected in futuristic mirrored walls. The stylish and intelligent hub of the city shows such flair and panache that one wonders if it is not perhaps due to divine guidance from the Muse of Kansas City (center). Her statue stands at the gateway to downtown, where she casts her net among the dreams of men and brings many to fruition.

boats to Baptists. Linked by walkways to the classic Art Deco Municipal Auditorium and complemented in function by the Kemper Arena a mile to the west, Bartle assures the city a vigorous convention industry.

One senses a special excitement in downtown Kansas City, an irrepressible optimism about the central city's future. The new Golden Age has already begun based on business and finance, government and entertainment — a new downtown design for a new American need.

From any of downtown's choice upper floors, hummocks, or cliffs, you can get a compass-point view of the landscape. Downtown is not on the edge of the area's compass, but pivots the needle.

If you look first to the west and northwest, you will see another city across the state line in Wyandotte County — Kansas City, Kansas, its skyline and grain elevators a backdrop for the confluence of the rivers, the Missouri and the Kansas, which natives call the Kaw. These waterways spawned the city and still give it life.

The bottomland there boasts of the stockyards, famed for its steaks, cattle pens, crafty commission men, the activity at the Livestock Exchange, and the American Royal. One of America's leading livestock and horse shows, it is now handsomely housed in one of America's leading architectural showpieces — the award-winning Kemper Arena. Upstream on the Kaw, in places like Argentine and Turner, railroad yards and soap factories, regional centers for food and mail distribution claim river frontage.

North of downtown, the muddy Missouri defines the boundary between the states of Kansas and Missouri. In the big Fairfax industrial district upstream on the Kansas side, grain from riverbank elevators is loaded onto barges bound for New Orleans. Fairfax is a place of petroleum refineries and storage, of plants that produce new Buicks, Oldsmobiles and Pontiacs, fiberglass, mattresses and cookies.

Everywhere people raise monuments expressive of themselves. Kansas Citians preserve their sense of history in a lordly bronze sculpture of General Andrew Jackson. They remember their beefsteak beginnings and cattle economy in a resolute and uniquely midwestern cast of a giant Hereford bull. Their gaiety is echoed in the ebullience of a downtown fountain. They honor their number one citizen, the scrappy "man from Independence," as they unveil his statue in the town square. And lastly they build big-muscled buildings with broad backs and proud stances, like the four-and-a-half-acre H. Roe Bartle Exposition Hall that hugs downtown's western horizon. They perch the marvelous Kemper Arena, like a gigantic, white, extraterrestrial insect with gleaming exoskeleton intact, among the Herefords and Angus in the West Bottoms. As Carl Sandburg said:
"They have made these steel skeletons like themselves – Lean, tumultuous, restless: They have put up tall witnesses, to fade in a cool midnight blue, to rise in evening rainbow prints...."

Centuries ago, artists discovered that even a common horse trough could be beautiful. The Greeks, and particularly the Romans, sculpted upon these troughs friezes of animals, fauns and faces, and during the Renaissance great artists and sculptors developed these formerly mundane, utilitarian troughs into works of great and lasting beauty.

Thus, the fountain. Fountains are a unique art form blending sight with sound and movement, together with a sense of touch, to create inspiring hymns of inspiration.

Kansas City has long recognized the fascination of bubbling water – at least since the 1920s, when developer J. C. Nichols imported more than $1 million worth of art, including fountains, to beautify his Country Club Plaza and residential area. Today many of our parks and boulevards – and even the downtown area – are graced by fountains.

This legacy of attention to the beautiful aspects of city living is destined to continue in Kansas City. The City of Fountains Foundation, a private group of citizens, has launched a continuous fund raising campaign from local individuals and companies to build a fountain a year.

A Kansas City landmark, the J. C. Nichols Memorial Fountain is one of more than fifty art treasures adorning the Country Club Plaza.

North, past the cornmeal and flour mills, past the Co-op research and the popcorn processing, are the rolling hills of both Clay and Platte counties. Quality homes are there along with fine schools and a genuine rural setting.

Northeast a compass point or two sprawls sports tycoon Lamar Hunt's Worlds of Fun amusement park. In the same vicinity lie underground quarries that have been turned into climate-controlled warehouses for the city's foreign trade zone operation.

Spread out in an easterly direction, mostly out of downtown view, vital industries break the landscape: Brobdingnagian assembly plants for Fords, Chevrolets, and giant Dart and Kenworth trucks; industries that make steel cable and barbed wire, prefabricated metal buildings, and agricultural chemicals; a petroleum refinery; and a huge coal-powered power plant.

Directly east and south of downtown lies the inner city, still an area of single family dwellings and yards where close-in industrial parks, housing projects, and renovation spark a renewed hope, a growing pride in community. Farther to the east is the Harry S. Truman Sports Complex — two, not one, Age of Aquarius stadiums, side by side — one for baseball, one for football. Still farther east is Independence, site of the presidential library, home, and favorite haunts of the area's best-known figure — Harry S. Truman. It is an old city, a model of Middle America: frame houses with porches, swings, and gabled bedrooms.

As you turn toward the south of downtown Kansas City, on another hill about a mile away, you can see further proof of the variety of parts that blend into the fascinating total picture. Here Hallmark Cards is building its version of Utopia — Crown Center. By late century, more than 8,000 people will be living in this model urban community of offices, shops, restaurants, hotels, residences, and pocket parks.

Farther south, the Country Club Plaza, more

than fifty years old, continues to awe visitors. One of the world's most sophisticated retail-residential communities, the Plaza is a source of great pride locally. Set in architecture styled after the ornate and picturesque cities of the Iberian Peninsula, quality is its byword.

The city's patricians have traditionally lived near the Plaza, and it is still true today. Nowhere in America has sound planning for residential beauty borne such fruit as in Jesse Clyde Nichols' Country Club District. Towering trees mix with majestic homes to elevate the eye, lift the spirit.

West of the Plaza is Johnson County in Kansas, one of the nation's richest counties. For miles of winding streets, carefully planned and stringently zoned towns with Old West names such as Mission Hills, Prairie Village, and Overland Park nestle against one another, unspoiled for the most part by neon strips and hasty structures of dubious value. This sixty-three square miles is the world's largest residential area of quality and comfort, space and beauty.

And so the "tour" ends. As a modern place in a changing world, Kansas City was slow to alter its serene setting and almost too cozy life-style. Awakened, it now seems to lead the revolt against the domineering dictates of long-powerful eastern cities. The rolling hills now harbor the nation's finest residential districts, with Prussian-tough zoning and an enviable quality of life. Carefully planned Kansas City International Airport, for example, is buffered by so much city land that the whining jets will never descend over homes or schools, yet the trend-setting, open-circle terminals are less than thirty minutes from downtown.

It is in agribusiness, distribution, transportation, and the service industries that Greater Kansas City sees its future. With the unnerving prospect of energy decreasing in supply and increasing in cost, Kansas City's centrality and proximity to fuel sources become geographic blessings. And as global needs for food increase, the cool, careful appraisers believe Kansas City is uniquely destined to serve its region, its nation, and emerging world markets.

But there is still more to this place, this Kansas City. It boasts a midland openness that welcomes the sky into daily life. The view above is always lively. It lowers itself at night onto the hillocks to enchant loyal patio sitters; it performs seasonal tricks with wind clouds, thunderheads, and wispy puffs; and it lays all aside to usher in its sun. With an innocence born of total dominance, the sky shares its ire and fury, wind and wickedness with the place below.

All seasons come to Kansas City in full measure. The dark of winter begins the year, enduring into March. Spring comes early, usually before all the firewood is burned. Summer stretches into late fall, broken by two or three searing seventy-two-hour stretches of withering dormancy when nothing alive moves with pleasure. Then, to the joy of poets, Indian summer resumes the rhythm of the seasons, appearing first in the tips of the oak leaf and proving anew that green converts into any color seen in a western sunset.

Kansas City, then, owes its character to natural science and the whimsies of nature; its setting of rock, woods, and bluffs; its full membership in each of the seasons. Much the same might be said of any city, but here, all seems moderate and in just proportions.

Nature's influence, weather aside, was determined geologically eons before, and the result has been a joy. Nature's weather governs our daily comings and goings, gracing life with color and variety. But nature's role is largely done.

Kansas City must look now to the hands, the heads, and the hearts of humans for physical change. It must look inward toward its own, as it always has since the days when the West was found — and the city founded — by rock-ribbed stalwarts named Chouteau, McCoy and Van Horn.

Fountains: they are a Kansas City hallmark. Few cities in the world can boast the water artistry that graces the boulevards, parks, and centers here. Herbert Silverman was amazed when he completed the aqua pura *tour. Afterwards, he wrote for* Travel and Leisure:

"In the order of magnitude of citizens' pride – one must marvel first at its fountains. New York has fountains and so has Rome, but Kansas City is deluged with them.

"Walk first through the fountains of Country Club Plaza....There are small fountains, large fountains, curving fountains. There is statuary above water, underwater, alongside water....

"The venerable Kansas City Star *has oblong fountains, and the new Alameda Plaza Hotel has fountains, but it also has a waterfall. Sculptor Carl Milles' last major work is a fountain. It rises beside an art museum, the Nelson Gallery....*

"Crown Center Hotel may have the most remarkable lobby background in the country – 'a series of waterfalls cascading 60 feet down an indoor hillside.' Crown Center already has a fountain that can weave geometric patterns in water, at the rate of 3,500 gallons a minute....

"The baseball stadium...also has a fountain. This one includes a 70-foot geyser that goes up and down with the roar of the crowds....

"And what an airport has landed in K.C.! It makes Kennedy and O'Hare look shabby and outmoded. ...it doesn't have a fountain, it has a lake!"

In 1832 Washington Irving looked out over the Kansas City hills and confided to his journal: "The fertility of all this Western country is truly astonishing. The soil is like that of a garden, and the luxuriance and the beauty of the forests exceed any that I have seen."

Joseph Smith, the Mormon prophet, waxed eloquent, convinced that he had found a promised land: "Unlike the timbered states in the East, except on the river and water courses which were virtually dotted with trees from one to three miles wide, so far as the eye can glance, the beautiful rolling prairies spread around like a sea of meadows.... The prairies were decorated with a growth of flowers which seemed as gorgeous and grand as the brilliancy of the stars in the heavens and exceed description....The season is mild and delightful three quarters of the year and...it bids fair to become one of the most blessed places on the globe."

In all the intervening years, little of this natural scenic beauty has been lost. Indeed, through creative landscaping, planting and civic pride, much of Kansas City's beauty has been greatly enhanced. There is yet much to delight the eye and lift man's thoughts to comparisons with the brilliancy of the stars in the heavens.

19

The russet fire of fall tints the maple leaves in Kansas City. Winter transforms her fields to swards of ermine. Spring brings the first coy beckonings of renewal and rebirth. Summer stands lovely in her lush green. But such is true almost anywhere. What is private to Kansas City is the way her people observe the seasons.

To some, spring comes with the first barge to dock at Kansas City on its way downriver. April 1 marks the traditional opening of the Missouri. To others spring will await the discovery of the first patch of morel mushrooms, a local delicacy pursued with unremitting zeal.

Summer is heralded by waving wheat fields and colonnades of Midwest corn. Soon fishermen will set off angling for that peculiar Missouri native, the spoon-bill catfish. Idyllic, yes. But caution: this is also the season when sultry afternoons foretell of violent storms, sometimes twisters boiling up out of the south, barreling up "tornado alley."

There is no other word for fall than "football." Big Eight partisans get their dander up. Chiefs fans outfitted in red "wolfpack" jackets seem as numerous as autumn leaves. Their numbers are legion.

Winter sees the opera and philharmonic seasons well under way. The city's many fountains support an army of ice skaters, each convinced that the meager twenty-inch annual snowfall makes for "a very hard winter."

And some, of course, talk with happy anticipation of the weeks to come, a favorite mushroom patch to prospect, the fortunes of the baseball team...and the first barge to churn downriver.

20

From the early 1800s when buffalo hides, grain, and gold first lured men up the river they called "Old Misery," the port of Kansas City has looked out on an unbroken procession of various kinds of boats and boatmen. A hundred years ago, great canoes fifty feet long lurched under the double burden of families and household goods. Arks – massive, thick-planked broadhorns, the water bugs of the river – scuttled past, poled by mud-caked rivermen.

With the migration of the Mormons and the influx of gold-fevered forty-niners, river traffic swelled to a flood heralding "the golden age of the Missouri." These were called the "Kansas days of 1850" when the ornate and gilded river pilots, the gaudiest men on the river, pulled $900 a trip. They were busy and bustling times when over sixty boats traveled regularly between St. Louis and Kansas City, days when this town harbored no less than thirty tramp boats and packets and welcomed 729 ships in a single season.

The packets and keelboats are gone now, but freight still moves on the river, increasing year by year. A spokesman for the Army Corps of Engineers put the average yearly freight run along our stretch of river at 3.25 million tons. Fourteen barge companies serve Kansas City with eighteen landings in the metropolitan area. Big red hopper barges dock full of yellow Midwest corn. Others tow a season's worth of wheat to millers on the Illinois, Tennessee, and Ohio waterways. Up and down the river, men load cargoes of molasses, paper, and petrochemicals. With the development of modern barge techniques, the river is enjoying an important renaissance. Industry officials are seeing substantial growth as a newly dredged nine-foot channel along the entire stretch of river assures a second "golden age" for the Missouri.

23

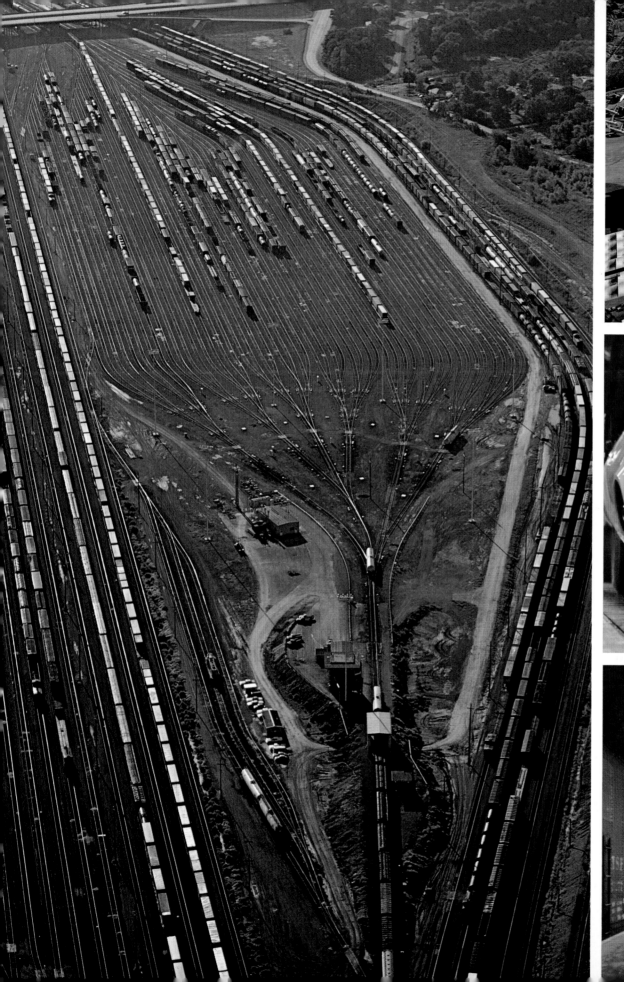

Land at Kansas City's breathtaking International Airport, and we'll wager it's the first time you walked as short a distance as eighty-five feet from the plane to your car.

Although the metropolitan area ranks twenty-ninth in population, national firsts are becoming routine. Kansas City is first in greeting card publishing and envelope production. Its foreign trade zone, the first in midcontinent America, is the largest in the country.

Down at the Board of Trade, the busiest commodities exchange outside of Chicago, they are well aware that Kansas City leads in hard winter wheat marketing. And thanks to cathedral-size limestone caverns, Kansas City is first in underground storage space and frozen storage and distribution.

Now for some more surprises: Kansas City is third in combined car and truck production, though all you've ever heard about is a place called Detroit. Drawing on the rich agricultural region surrounding it, Kansas City is first among the nation's cities in overall farm equipment distribution and second in wheat flour production and grain elevator capacity. At the crossroads of America, Kansas City plays an important role as the nation's third largest rail center and freight car handler.

TWA, Hallmark Cards, and the university system are among the city's top employers. So are Sears, J.C. Penney, Montgomery Ward, Sony, and Toyota, all of whom service the central United States from distribution centers here. Big-muscled industries like General Motors, Bendix, Western Electric, Ford, Remington Arms, Armco Steel, and Allis-Chalmers have also found homes in nearby industrial parks.

And Kansas City has the financial clout to keep its industry in high gear. It is the number eleven center of correspondent banking in the country and headquarters for one of the nation's twelve Federal Reserve Banks.

The West is Found

"Since the days of Columbus, commerce and enterprise have been seeking the West — west, west has ever been the watchword — over the Atlantic, up the Potomac, across the Alleghenies, down the Ohio, over the Mississippi, up the Missouri. It is found at last. Kansas City stands on the extreme western point of navigation — it is *the* West of commerce; beyond us the West must come to us overland. I say again — the West at last is found!"

Not a person in the room would have dared doubt it for a second, as Robert Thompson Van Horn — editor, future mayor and congressman, and already a civic booster *par excellence* — lifted his glass to toast the wildly cheering, applauding crowd on Christmas Day of 1857. These were citizens who had linked their own hopes and dreams to the future of this yet unpolished community at the wild western edge of Missouri. They had gathered to raise civic and personal spirits through the strength of sympathetic numbers and to celebrate the promise of success they had always known was imminent.

It might have happened just that way. Kansas City in the 1850s was a community of anywhere from a few hundred to almost five thousand people, depending on which account and which year you consider. By 1857, the year in which Van Horn delivered the above panegyric of manifest midwestern destiny, the town had a history of no more than thirty-six years. And they had been hard years, caked with the mud of the uncivilized prairie, soiled with the sweat and tears that came with trying to tame it.

It had been tamed, to a point. Only four decades earlier, the place where Van Horn and his listeners sat enjoying their good fortune had been deep forests where Osage and Kansas Indians enjoyed the prosperity of good hunting, with the same prosperity in fishing available in the nearby rivers.

A decade later, Francois Chouteau and his band of French fur traders had already found Van Horn's "West of commerce." They had settled once — in 1821 — between what are now Independence and Kansas City, but the predictably unpredictable Missouri River had flooded her banks and wiped out Chouteau's small community. Thus watered, the seed that was one day to become a civilized Kansas City flowed three miles west and took firmer root: Chouteau rebuilt his fur warehouse near the great bend of the river at what is now the foot of Grand Avenue. But Chouteau's interest was in fur trading, not city building. The seed he planted remained dormant for a number of years while this small band of Frenchmen happily pursued their own limited, immediate goals.

In the 1830s American traders were following a well-beaten trail to Santa Fe, the capital of New Mexico, where they had found an enthusiastic and lucrative market for their wares. Independence, Missouri, was the main outfitting point.

Ancient artifacts uncovered in the Kansas City area reveal that Indians may have lived here as far back as ten thousand years ago, according to archaeologist J. Mett Shippee of the Smithsonian Institution.

The first Indians were nomads who roamed what are now Jackson, Clay, and Platte counties. Later, during the so-called Archaic period, Indians settled in villages and became adept hunters and gardeners.

A culture known as the Mississippian was here from A.D. 800 to A.D. 1300. The Indians are thought to have migrated from settlements along the Mississippi River. They relied on hunting, gathering, and gardening to supply their food. They lived in large villages at first, then spread out into the wilderness to set up smaller camps.

After A.D. 1300 no evidence of Indians is found in Kansas City, although the Missouri, Osage, and Kansas tribes had villages fifty miles away.

Clockwise, from the upper left:
Stone axes, typical of those found on Nebo Hill sites of 5,000 B.C. and earlier.
Pottery made by Mississippians.
A polished diorite.
Spear points used by Indians before 4,000 B.C.
Arrow points – A.D. 500 to 800.
Dark flint – 8,000 to 10,000 B.C.
Spear points – 500 B.C. to A.D. one.
Combination knife-scraper made of flint.
Rim section of a classic Hopewell vessel.

At top right is a painting of Kansas Chief White Plume; far right, a Kansas woman dressed in the tribe's traditional garb; and below, a war dance in a Kansas lodge

But the wily son of a Baptist missionary changed that. John C. McCoy, easily Kansas City's first entrepreneur, saw a chance to make a profit by opening an outfitters store four miles south of the French river settlement in a place called Westport. This outfitting point, if used by the traders, would shorten the overland route to Santa Fe.

In the entrepreneurial vernacular, McCoy "ran with it." Not only did he open a store — which still stands today as Kelly's, one of Kansas City's more popular saloons — McCoy cut a road through the dense forest to a natural rock levee near where Chouteau was still dealing in furs, oblivious to the wider trading opportunities that McCoy sensed. McCoy's goods would arrive at the levee by boat, and then he would have them brought over this more direct route to his store.

The scheme worked. Westport supplanted Independence as an outfitting point, and this little clearing in the Missouri wilderness eventually became a full-fledged frontier town — with continued help from McCoy, the eternal promoter, who platted the land into a township and sold lots. To anyone who agreed to build in Westport, McCoy gave the lots free.

In 1838 McCoy's business acumen became focused on the other end of his four-mile wagon trail. An early settler named Gabriel Prudhomme had built up a 257-acre farm by the river. When Prudhomme was killed in a barroom fight, his farm — advertised as "one of the best steamboat landings on the Missouri River" — was put up for public auction. Acting quickly, McCoy organized — with thirteen other men — the Kansas Town Company, and for $4,220 they bought the hilly farm that became downtown Kansas City.

When history buffs discuss the *founding* of Kansas City, they always speak of John McCoy; but when they discuss the *naming* of the city, McCoy's prominence pales beside that of a colorful pioneer character with the unforgettable name of "One-Eyed Ellis." In the words of historian Darrell Garwood, after the Kansas Town

The first white man to settle in the Kansas City area was Francois Chouteau. In 1821 he brought his family here to found a modest fur-trading post. The land along the river hardly needed to be cleared to make room for the solitary warehouse and small cluster of dwellings.

Life was hard. Chouteau and his family worked long hours and prayed by candlelight, celebrating mass at home. Slowly the outpost grew and other Frenchmen settled here. They gave their names to river bends and crossings: Rivard, Prudhomme, and Laliberte. Even the word "prairie" was theirs.

The settlers traded with fur trappers and rivermen. Already traffic up the Missouri had begun to swell. Fifty-foot canoes and big Kentucky broadhorns brought immigrant families and cargoes of furs. According to one resident: "The Canadian-French were making more than a living feeding and rooming the hunters and trappers and selling garden products to the fur boats and to men passing in skiffs....Nature had made a good landing place...and soldiers... would go to the Canadian squatters for potatoes, chickens and prairie birds and sometimes make contracts for a regular supply for the army. Money was passing hands and a few stores were doing good business...."

By the 1840s brick houses began to supplant the rude lean-tos and trappers' shanties. Men began to fence the land relinquished first by the Indian, then by the trapper. Author Rufus Sage was there and saw the beginning of the end. He said simply, "The country in this vicinity is beginning to be generally settled by thrifty farmers."

Company had bought the Prudhomme farm at auction, "...they immediately retired to discuss their plans before a hickory fire in a place kept by a lanky, cadaverous character known as 'One-Eyed Ellis.' Gathered in his cabin near the levee, the founders selected their host to preside over their meeting. Ellis was not a member of the Town Company, but he sometimes acted as a Justice of the Peace when a sale of livestock or other transaction requiring a signature was completed on the levee, and this faint connection with legal procedure seemed to make his chairmanship appropriate.

"The chairmanship of the first meeting of the founders caused One-Eyed Ellis to become associated with the story of Kansas City. Otherwise he would have remained obscure in his cabin under the bluff, where he gained his living in part from the illegal sale of firewater to the Indians. From the door of his cabin, with his one good eye, he kept a sharp lookout for Indians and squatters with whom he might trade a tin cup of whisky for a coonskin — a very profitable trade, since a coonskin was worth about fifty cents in St. Louis, and the whisky he dispensed was wholesaling at fifteen cents a gallon. He also augmented his income occasionally by catching a stray horse or steer.

"As chairman of the meeting, One-Eyed Ellis got out a blue-backed Webster's spelling book and leafed through it in the hope of coming upon a word that would make a good name for the new town. He apparently found nothing that appealed to the founders in the general discussion which followed. Certain of the founders later recalled that Abraham Fonda, one of their number, who wore a tail coat and liked to record his occupation as 'gentleman,' was insistent that the town should be called 'Port Fonda'; and that someone else said he would prefer 'Rabbitville' or 'Possum Trot.' But finally, after a good deal of bantering, they chose the name 'Kansas,' an Indian word which meant 'smoky wind' and was used to designate prairie fires. It was also the name of an Indian tribe native to the vicinity."

Cities are seldom built intentionally; rather, they grow as by-products of their unwitting builders' selfish motives. Then one day the builder looks up and realizes that the city has swallowed both him *and* his motive. His well-being now depends on the city's, so he has to take care of it.

Probably no one during that early period in Kansas City's life had civic concerns on his mind. After all, the underlying premise of westward expansion was that you could still score big *somewhere* in all that virgin land.

John McCoy and company *were* scoring big. Between 1839 and the early 1850s, Westport and "Kansas" erupted and formed the boundaries of what became one of the hottest four-mile business booms on the frontier.

The Indian fur trade, though dwindling and eventually fading in the 1840s, had brought ambitious men to this western gateway, many of whom had made a good deal of money. Chouteau was gone by 1845, but many others had developed frontier fever and stayed to put their money into something else.

All over the eastern half of America, hopeful men were heeding Horace Greeley's advice to "go west," and rough-edged settlements like Kansas and Westport were ready to help them on their western way. Commodity trading with the Indians, warehousing and transferring goods bound for Santa Fe, the outfitting of emigrants to California and Oregon — these were the burgeoning businesses that made their owners wealthy and gave Kansas and Westport enough local color to keep both a Bret Harte and a Mark Twain busy for a couple of prolific lifetimes.

To call these places *cities* would be ludicrous; to call them *towns* may be pushing it. They were really outposts, with an accent on *out*. Quite literally, Kansas and Westport were the jumping-off places of America.

It's not hard to imagine either place, with Westport only a slightly more populous version of

Typified by the crusty appearance of its first town hall (top right), Westport was one of those contentious and dedicated little towns that made the American frontier indomitable and unique. In 1836 there were only fifty persons living here, but among them was John Sutter, later of California gold fame. Westport seemed far away from civilization, and yet it was as close as men like Kit Carson and Jim Bridger cared to get.

By the forties, pioneer businessman John McCoy (lower right) had made the town a robust part of western economy, sharing in the profits of Indian fur trade, traffic in buffalo hides, and outfitting wagons bound for Santa Fe and Oregon. Indians, Mexicans, and mountain men gave the place rustic color. Buffalo hunters wandered the streets as shaggy and bellicose as their prey. Mule skinners and drovers cracking Loudon County blacksnake whips dazzled the eyes of small boys and local loafers. Sometimes a trader would pull in with as much as $100,000 in Mexican silver, making for a beguiling mixture of the elegant and rough and ready.

Already there was a rivalry between Independence and the Westport area. Rufus Sage watched these upstart prairie towns through their youth and wrote: "Situated as they are, at the utmost verge of civilization, and upon the direct route to Oregon and regions adjacent, they must retain and command, as the starting points for emigrants and traders, that importance already assumed by general consent."

Later, Westport, because of its plentiful grazing for wagon oxen, began to supplant Independence as an embarkation point for the west. In 1850 a resident was able to boast, "All the noise here is people getting ready for California – mules and other stock is high." George Fuller Green captures this hustle and bustle in his painting Main Street Westport *(lower far right).*

Kansas: muddy trails connecting one rude wooden building to another, and, crowding these trails, wagons and horses and oxen and men, all manner of men — veritable extensions of the wilderness that bred them. The flow of liquor apparently rivaled that of the Missouri River itself. As one historian described the situation, "Whiskey circulated more freely...than was altogether safe in a place where every man carried a loaded pistol...."

But business was brisk, and it appeared that the most money was to be made in the exchange of goods from one holder to another. Because of its more advantageous river location, Kansas began to overtake Westport in the late 1840s. In 1846 seven hundred steamboats unloaded passengers and goods. The next year, the first wagon train to leave from *Kansas*, not Westport, headed out toward Santa Fe. In 1850 some six hundred wagon trains — many no doubt chasing the dream of California gold — originated in the bustling river community. That same year, total business for the town of Kansas hit the $5 million mark.

If California offered the promise of gold, this hilly river town on the edge of civilization offered a future of golden promise. As Van Horn would soon say, the West at last was found.

Cities are like children: they both start off raucous and undisciplined, shortsighted, impulsive, selfish, and a little bit messy. Eventually, though, they mature if they are to survive.

By the early 1850s Kansas City's childhood was coming to an end, and signs of maturity were beginning to show. At the start of the decade, the people living in the river settlement had felt enough singleness of purpose to lead them to petition for town organization. The county court granted the charter making Kansas the Town of Kansas, and a loose system of trusteeship was quickly set up to carry out the will of the community. The first order of business was the establishment of a small police force — a sure signal that civilization was landing on the levee.

The representation above, of the city of Kansas was drawn for the Pictorial by Mr. Kilburn, the view being taken on the spot, and executed with his accustomed fidelity. The city is in Jackson County, Missouri, and is located on the south bank of the Missouri river, one hundred and thirty miles from Jefferson City. It is a place of considerable business, and embraces all the elements of future greatness. We present it as it appears today, but the cities of the West grow out of all recognition in a very few years. In the old world, the view of a town taken today would exhibit few changes from one a century old—the little settlements on the Rhine, for instance, are quite stationary—while rapid expansion and perpetual improvement are the features of our settlements, particularly in the great West, which is dotted here and there with foci of life and business, often a marvel even to us of New England, with whom progress and extension are the watchwords.

The Weekly Border Star.

DEVOTED TO
LITERATURE, POLITICS AND NEWS.

POSTAGE ON THE BORDER STAR.

Within Jackson county,	Free.
Within Missouri, per year,	13 cts.
Anywhere within the States or Territories,	26 cts.

WESTPORT, MO.,
FRIDAY MORNING, - - - - - - FEB. 25.

The Point to Start From.

We tell our Kentucky friends and other Eastern men who are thinking of going to the gold mines, that they will be humbugged if they go farther up the Missouri river than the mouth of the Kansas. Every mile they go up the Missouri after they get to Kansas City will be just so much out of their way. Kansas City is *the starting point.* This is evident to every one who is acquainted with the geography and thoroughfares of the western country, and those who advise you to start from any other point either have been deceived or are trying to deceive. There is no mistake about this matter, else we would not speak so positively.

Our readers know that we never mislead or deceive them. They know that we are no puffer of any town or interest, and that we have never awarded to Kansas City more than she deserved. We own no property there, and have no *inducement* to puff her. But truth is truth and justice is justice—and both truth and justice require us to tell the gold-seekers that they will save time and money by *making Kansas City their starting point.*

34

Drunks, border ruffians, and renegades peopled the muddy streets of Kansas City in the 1850s. As Henry C. Haskell and Richard B. Fowler point out in the book City of the Future, they were right at home in the bedraggled and woefully scrofulous surroundings of the infant river town:

"The ground upon which it stood sloped up from the river, gradually at first, then steeply. The inhabited area contained a jumble of frame shacks, interspersed with a few more substantial brick buildings near the levee and thinning out, as the terrain became more difficult. Here and there houses clung precariously to the wall of the valley. The city offered no common conveniences of any kind. Its streets were alternately mud bogs or ankle-deep in dust. Water for washing had to be 'toted' by pail. Drinking water was almost unobtainable. Other beverages, however, do not appear to have been in such short supply. Kansas City, which had only about 2,000 permanent residents, possessed several dozen saloons. As for gambling houses, well, it was a river town."

Hardships and hard liquor notwithstanding, the New England Pictorial and local Border Star (both left) blithely boasted that Kansas City was the gateway west, a gateway embracing "all the elements of future greatness."

Settlers went westward from Kansas City in droves. The trek to Santa Fe, Oregon, and California was accomplished in the venerable, whale-bellied, wide-wheeled Conestoga wagon. Words might describe the detail: the starboard side buckets of tar for lubrication, the red running gear, wrenches, gimlets, and wagon tools. But words cannot do justice to the determination of the driver nor the broad-chested majesty of his four-ox team laboring in brassbound harness.

Where words pale, the robust vigor of Thomas Hart Benton's murals shines. This view is northeasterly up the Missouri River where wagon trains slogged in toward Council Bluffs. The covered wagons, the mountain man, and Indian trader shown here speak eloquently of the day when Kansas City was the Gateway to the West.

The first wagon train to leave directly from Kansas City for the Southwest was assembled in 1847. By 1850, six hundred wagons pushed off across the prairie, including one giant convoy of ten wagons drawn by 130 oxen. "There are a great many Santa Feans now...busily preparing to set out on their journey across the plains," said a newspaper in 1851. "Those now here will leave in a few days, and we are glad to find that they are so numerous and so well armed as to rob the trip of most of its dangers."

And an enthusiastic correspondent for the Missouri Republican portrayed the city's advantages for west-bound pioneers:

"An excellent road leads from the river...to the open prairie....Wagons, mules, cattle, ponies, saddles, harness, grain, provisions, groceries — everything, in fact, necessary to the trip and the comfort of the immigrants, can be obtained...."

To create an uptown section accessible from the rock levee, streets were carved out of the north bluffs. Cuts up to forty feet were required, and the resulting canyons earned Kansas City the nickname "Gully Town." The unusual scene is portrayed in City of the Future: *"A newspaper correspondent reported that 'carts and horses wallowed in the mud of these excavations, and the houses stood trembling on the verge as if in fear of tumbling over.' From the point of view of the householder the situation must sometimes have been a trifle disconcerting. For example, a Dr. Thomas B. Lester had maintained an office in his cottage on Main Street between Second and Third. When the city fathers graded Main down ten feet in front, he underbuilt a second story, to keep his business quarters at the street level. They then excavated another twelve feet. Whereupon, the good doctor, nothing daunted, put a third floor beneath his original house, thus ending up with a three-story building, constructed literally from top to bottom."*

Three reasons why Kansas City richly deserved the nickname "Gully Town": A canyon of grand proportions divided two banks on Second Street in 1869 (top), while nearby at Second and Delaware emigrants camped (bottom left). The southeast corner of Third and Delaware (bottom right) was no place for a house in 1868, but one was perched there anyway – a sign of the precarious times.

There were other signs. Transients were just beginning to enjoy the town's first hotel, which was vigorously advertised as being "roomy and modern." And for a few months in 1851, hotel guests were able to read in the Kansas *Public Ledger*, the first local newspaper, what a progressive and dynamic community they were visiting. The *Ledger* shut down undynamically after only a few issues.

But there would be other newspapers, other hotels. And another city name, as well. In 1853 — in anticipation of the onslaught of people and commodity traffic that could be imminent as a result of the recent opening of the Nebraska and Kansas territories to the west — the increasingly farsighted town fathers of Kansas needed the more sophisticated benefits of *city* government. They applied to the state general assembly, and on Washington's Birthday, 1853, the Town of Kansas became Kansas City.

Names are names. The young city still didn't look like anyplace you'd want to hang your hopes on — much less your hat, if that meant staying. For one thing, there were those infernal bluffs. With the opening of the West, rivalry among border towns was keen, and Kansas City was known derisively in some of the competitive communities as "Gully Town." The name fit the topography: how could a city's people see eye-to-eye when some lived in gullies and some on hills? And could even the most persuasive frontier flimflam man sell an investor on the idea of putting up his store on a seventy-degree slope? Kansas City may well have been the birthplace of that corny old joke about "business falling off."

But business wasn't, not in Kansas City. The recently emerged spirit of *community* wouldn't let it. The hotels, the newspapers, the urge to build streets and banks and all the rest — these were the outward signs of the maturity spoken of earlier. But the seat of that maturity was in the changing attitude among citizens — an attitude which no longer reflected the vagrant self-purpose of the early settlers but rather, in the early 1850s, began to emphasize the value of collective well-being. It was this community spirit that enabled Kansas City to overcome almost any obstacle it encountered during the next two decades on its way to becoming a true regional metropolis.

During the first year of city government, Kansas City took in less than three hundred dollars in taxes; by 1856 the figure had jumped to one thousand dollars annually. That same year the first bank opened for business, the Board of Trade was established, and the levee was paved.

A year later, the City Council opened and graded several streets from the levee south, including Grand Avenue, Walnut, Main, Delaware, and Wyandotte streets. A chamber of commerce was formed, and stagecoach routes were mapped. Telegraph communication linked the settled East with the frontier. The East got the message: Kansas City's economic base broadened to include dry goods and meat-packing firms. And down on the levee the people kept coming, with between five and ten steamboats per day emptying their charges of wide-eyed humanity eager to get on with the western experience. The Gillis House, a riverfront hotel, had twenty-seven thousand guests in 1857 — nearly all of them settlers bound for Kansas.

If any one concern must be singled out to characterize the Kansas City of the 1850s and 1860s, it has to be the rush for the railroad. Which heartland city would become the rail gateway from East to West?

Chartering railroad companies became a sort of civic pastime in Kansas City, though most such organizations and plans eventually became derailed at various points along the way. And when a Kansas territorial official suggested to an eastern industrialist the possibility of a railroad link near Kansas City, the easterner reportedly shook his head in wonderment at the folly of the midwestern fools and replied thusly: "My dear sir, I beg of you, for your sake and that of your promising town, you will never again make your last observation to anyone else. I can excuse your

The Kansas City of the 1870s was an unprepossessing place of quagmire streets and tobacco-stained boardwalks. Its scruffy appearance notwithstanding, this was a "Renaissance city."

The seventies were periods of sobering droughts. In 1874 swarms of Rocky Mountain locusts descended like a biblical plague. By 1875 Missouri Governor Hardin felt compelled to proclaim a day of prayer for deliverance from the grasshoppers that had piled up several feet deep. No sooner had the proclamation been issued than the locusts miraculously flew off in clouds that darkened the sky.

At the same time, six thousand Mennonites arrived from Russia with a new and hardy variety of wheat called "Turkey Red." This strain proved enormously successful and launched the Midwest toward preeminence in the world's grain market.

Beef was also big business. And with the cattle came the cowboys, gamblers, and gunmen who changed the life-style of the town. Darrell Garwood writes:

"Kansas City became a capital of cow towns....Wild Bill Hickok and other well-known gunmen were all familiar figures. These gunmen were the celebrities of the day, and their personalities were much better known than those of the residents on Quality Hill. Wild Bill Hickok...lived three years in Kansas City, and walked every day to play faro at the Marble Hall."

Here are three views of the "capital of cow towns" in its heyday. The famous Marble Hall is visible in the picture taken north along Main Street (top). Walnut Street appears to be wallowing in mud (lower right) as does the south part of Main (far right).

enthusiasm, but others may not. Your steamboats are here, you will have a good town, perhaps a respectable city, but never in your day or your children's will a railroad reach, much less go to the west of you." He was wrong, of course. But not being part of it, he couldn't have known the force of the growing Kansas City Spirit, or the power inherent in the city's amazing single-mindedness toward bringing the railroad to fruition in Kansas City. This community spirit, seemingly lacking in competitive towns, must get much of the credit for eventually tipping the scales in Kansas City's favor.

And much of the credit for maintaining that community spirit must go to Robert T. Van Horn. In 1854 the small nucleus of business leadership realized that if Kansas City's natural and man-made advantages as an urban center were ever to be fully exploited, someone had to take the lead in telling the rest of the world about what Kansas City had to offer. That someone was Van Horn, a former newspaper editor in Ohio whom they found in St. Louis looking for a chance to make his mark. Van Horn liked what he heard about Kansas City. He blew into town in 1855 and immediately took charge of the *Enterprise*, the newspaper which soon became the public voice of the business community.

There were many prophecies being trumpeted about during those days concerning Kansas City's chances for future success. William Gilpin, Sen. Thomas Hart Benton, John C. Fremont, Charles Spalding — these, among others, were the acknowledged prophets who visualized greatness for this city at the confluence of the Missouri and Kansas rivers. And behind their prophecies lay always the main idea of *natural advantages*, which, with a bit of coaxing from the likes of Robert Van Horn, could easily be construed as a shining example of *manifest destiny*.

At the very same Christmas celebration during which Van Horn eulogized the "finding" of the West, he expressed — as he had done time and again in the pages of his newspaper — his pro-

found conviction that Kansas City was indeed the chosen city: "God has marked out by topography the lines of commerce, and it is by studying these great tracings of the Almighty's finger that the pioneer of trade and the herald of civilization has selected the site of those gigantic cities of the Republic, and which has fixed upon the rock-bound bay of the Missouri and Kansas as the last great seat of wealth...."

The building of this "seat of wealth," then, became Robert Van Horn's personal cause, and he was very much a respected part of those early city builders — Coates, McCoy, Lykins, Gillis, McGee, Campbell, Troost, Chick, Swope, Northrup — many of whose names today conjure images of street signs or city landmarks. Van Horn was never distracted from the best interest of the city. At home he stimulated civic pride by praising community accomplishments, and yet he continually editorialized for more hotels, graded streets and other refinements and, above all, for the avoidance of divisive politics that could endanger the city's chances of getting the railroad.

Both locally and around the country, in the newspaper — whose name he had changed to the *Western Journal of Commerce* — and on speaking trips, Van Horn delineated the doctrine of Kansas City's manifest destiny. He repelled the long-standing "Great American Desert" image of the newly opened western land by promoting Kansas City and the prairie across the river as one of America's garden spots. He bold-faced the good news and played down the bad; and whenever he could turn a piece of bad publicity to the business advantage, he did it.

Reports of the time indicate that there was much public sentiment against the number of saloons and the open drunkenness and frequent fights in the still-rough river town. In 1857 when one estimate of the population was a mere fifteen hundred, whiskey sales were an inebriating $135,000. Van Horn then suggested in his newspaper that the time was right for the establishment of some locally owned distilleries.

There were those who were sorry to see the billowy grace of the covered wagon give way to the stench and clatter of the first primitive, rawboned locomotive (right) to enter Kansas City. Others felt its cinders-and-soot presence would at last dispel the rough-and-tumbleweed image of the area (caricatured at far right) as the Great American Desert.

Mid-century saw three cities racing for railroad domination. Kansas City contrived to tap a northern rail line at Cameron and bottle up St. Joseph. But there were further difficulties.

Leavenworth, Kansas, was building its own line to Cameron. Charles Kearney, president of the Kansas City-Galveston line, maintained the slender legitimacy of his prior railroad contract. But he needed a bridge over the Missouri. Kearney's tactical tour de force which secured Kansas City's railroad supremacy is re-created in City of the Future:

"He telegraphed Kersey Coates... urging him also to proceed at once to Boston and hold off any proceedings in favor of Leavenworth....Coates promptly telegraphed R. T. Van Horn, who was now representing the Kansas City district in Congress....Van Horn had struck up a friendship with the chairman of the House committee on postoffices and post roads, which had river rights under its jurisdiction.... They drafted an amendment to include a bridge over the Missouri at Kansas City.

"The next day — with providence and some fast political footwork still on Kansas City's side — the amended bill was brought up on the floor of the House in the absence of any Kansas representative. Just as a member of the Kansas delegation rushed in with an amendment for another bridge at Leavenworth, Van Horn moved the previous question. Leavenworth's bid was too late....Kansas City had clinched its Chicago connection."

The period from the late 1850s through the mid 1860s was, of course, a trying time in Kansas City, just as it was in many areas of the United States. The slavery question was especially pointed in Kansas City, situated as the city was on the western edge of a predominantly slave state, just across the river from a statehood-bound territory whose stance on slavery was perhaps favoring the other foot.

And in the election of 1860, Kansas City found out some surprising facts about itself — among them that as a city grows, its mind becomes less and less predictable. The Kansas City votes in the presidential election broke down like this:

Stephen Douglas	487
John Bell	368
Abraham Lincoln	185
John C. Brekinridge	131

The very fact that Abraham Lincoln had received that many votes was disturbing to many townspeople because it pointed up a greater unrest. Eventually, the slavery question and the border trouble it spawned had profound effects on Kansas City: it caused violence which hurt business which in turn hurt some longtime friendships which disrupted the city's community spirit.

When war finally came, it crippled Kansas City. Business leaders whose dynamic single-mindedness had built a city were now facing one another across battle lines. Half the city's population packed up and left. The business boom was silenced. Westport, the threshold to the frontier where thousands of starry-eyed emigrants had anxiously prepared for the trip westward, now was filled with steel-eyed soldiers on their way to death in the bloody battle of Westport, known as the "Gettysburg of the West." Quantrill's Raiders rode — and at one point Quantrill actually captured the town of Independence. The Kansas City riverfront, once the threshold of booming business and relaxing bawdiness, now was the scene for the issuance of the infamous Order Number II, which exiled Confederate sympathizers and broke up many families.

The term "founding fathers" conjures up visions of armchair dons smiling down out of gilt-edged portraits. But the men who founded Kansas City were no fusty old attic relics. No, sir. They were mountain men, rumrunners and sodbusters. They were, like as not, tough-minded, tabasco-tongued sons of the frontier.

One was John McCoy, a barrel-chested son of a missionary. Another was Captain Bill Sublette, best of the mountain men. Called "Cut Face" by the Indians, he stood six feet two in his moccasins and was a man to be reckoned with. William Miles Chick and William Gillis counted for two more. They had come westward from the tidewater country where Gillis had already made a reputation as an Indian fighter. The founders numbered fourteen in all. Their purchase of the future city site was strictly a calculated risk. As McCoy said, they were "a few men with no capital...[who] bought the land because it had a good steamboat landing and was the most suitable starting point for...caravans to New Mexico. The idea that any one of them would live to see a city built...never entered into their calculation."

Darrell Garwood describes the sale itself: "The founding occurred on a cold November day in 1838. A chilling wind was blowing in off the river as a group of twenty-five or thirty fur-capped and booted men gathered on the levee for an auction....Captain Sublette...was selected to do the bidding for the Town Company. From time to time he raised a ham-like hand and offered a bid. He succeeded in purchasing the farm...at a price of $4,220."

Clockwise, from the upper left: Robert Van Horn; William Miles Chick; Johnston Lykins; Robert Campbell; William Gilpin; Kersey Coates; Benoist Troost; Hiram Northrup; Sen. Thomas Hart Benton; William Gillis.

General Order No. 11, issued by Brig. Gen. Thomas Ewing on August 25, 1863, from his headquarters at the old Pacific House in Kansas City, drove twenty thousand Missourians from their homes and inspired this angry painting by George Caleb Bingham, a Kansas City resident at the time. The infamous order remained in force until March 1864. Here is the text:

1) All persons living in Jackson, Cass and Bates counties, Missouri...are hereby ordered to remove from their present places of residence within fifteen days.... Those who within that time establish their loyalty to the Union to the satisfaction of the commanding officer of the military station nearest their present places of residence, will receive from him certificates stating the fact of their loyalty. ...All who receive such certificates will be permitted to remove to any military station in the district, or to any part of the state of Kansas, except the counties of the eastern border of the state. All others shall move out of this district....

2) All grain or hay...in the district from which the inhabitants are required to move...will be taken to military stations and turned over to the proper officers there, and report of the amount so turned over made to the district headquarters, specifying the names of all loyal owners and the amount of such produce taken from them. All grain and hay found in such district after the ninth of September next, not convenient to such stations, will be destroyed.

3) The provisions of General Order No. 10...will be vigorously executed...in parts of the district and at the stations not subject to the operation of paragraph one of this order, and especially in the towns of Westport, Independence and Kansas City.

4) Paragraph No. 3, General Order No. 10, is revoked as to all who have borne arms against the government in this district since the 20th of August 1863

The Battle of Westport (bottom left) marked the end of the Civil War in the West. Confederate troops under General Sterling Price were routed in a seesaw battle that saw superior Union forces turn both rebel flanks in drives by General Alfred Pleasonton and General Samuel Curtis.

Much of the battle raged around the stately brick mansion of John Wornall (top left), where his wife, Eliza, was alone with the children. For this family, the war had become a nightmare.

The slaves had gone and John had been impressed into a Kansas militia regiment. He would later say, not entirely without truth, that the battle was fought over Eliza's breakfast. At dawn, Confederates who had bivouacked south of the house came in and asked for food. No sooner had Eliza set the table than they were charged by Union soldiers who wolfed down everything. The rebel troops counterattacked with reinforcements and again Eliza fixed breakfast.

During the battle the Wornall House was used as a hospital by both sides. The Confederate wounded were brought there first. But when the Union forces began their final, successful push, rebel casualties were moved on and the federal wounded brought in.

Although the rebel army was effectively defeated and dispersed, there was no secure peace. Little knots of guerrillas remained, among them the James brothers, the Dalton gang, and Cole Younger.

Fortunately, the crippling effects of war were not permanent. Van Horn became mayor immediately after the war, and he began to urge concerted effort in the solving of problems left behind after the fighting.

A town that had sliced through eighty feet of river bluffs to make streets and overcome the sobriquet of Gully Town wasn't about to stop now. Enthusiasm was rekindled. The new editor of the paper alerted the world to Kansas City's reopening for business, and business reopened. Above all, the question of who would land the railroad link had not been settled, and between 1865 and 1869 competition among frontier towns such as Leavenworth, Lawrence, and Kansas City was renewed with all the spit and vigor of a saloon brawl.

Ultimately, Kansas City won. While business leaders in the other cities were fighting each other over just what was the best way to get the railroads, the Kansas City leadership stuck to a single line of attack and was able, with some quick-stepping in Congress, to present an attractive enough plan to convince the railroad people that Kansas City was indeed the right spot. So in July of 1869 the Hannibal Bridge, which brought the Hannibal and St. Joseph line from Chicago through Kansas City and was the first railroad bridge to connect the eastern side of the Missouri River with the west, was opened for traffic.

And on that day Kansas City turned out *en masse* to celebrate. Summertime and success: it was all beer and balloons and the happy words of self-congratulation, with that shining steel symbol of manifest *metropolitan* destiny looming high on the city's horizon.

This clinched it. In 1870 the federal census would put the Kansas City population figure at 32,260, when scarcely five years earlier the count had been a mere 3,500. And over the next decade the city — the *City* — would take shape, with a whole line of firsts: the stockyards, the Board of Trade Building, the Coates Opera House, the Kansas City Medical College, a stock exchange, a city hall, a criminal court, the Public Library, a telephone exchange, uniforms for police and firemen, an academy of science. Colorful and notorious characters like Wild Bill Hickok, Wyatt Earp, Jesse James, and Doc Holliday would mingle with wealthy and well-dressed people from all over the world who came to Kansas City to enjoy the wide-open, cosmopolitan delights of opera and theater, fine restaurants, and of course the all-night faro games of flamboyant Bob Potee, not to mention the unparalleled, refined-to-fit-the-times, European-elegance establishment of Madam Annie Chambers.

This is what waited on the other side of that bridge. But on that happy day in July 1869, the people of Kansas City were probably savoring the moment. It had been a long, long struggle, and as they enjoyed themselves a few hundred yards from where Francois Chouteau had started it all so many years before, they rejoiced in the comfortable feeling that one part of the struggle was over. The next day the newpaper headlined the Hannibal Bridge story with still another Kansas City prophecy: "KANSAS CITY FROM NOW ON WILL BOOM." As usual in Kansas City, probably no one doubted it for a second. Nor was there any reason to.

The building of the Hannibal Bridge marked a turning point in the history of Kansas City. It insured the primacy of the livestock business by opening a direct rail link with the big Chicago market, and it was a major factor in the opening of the West itself as over 260,000 settlers poured over the bridge in 1869, the first year of its completion.

But it was not a milestone reached without struggle. Kansas City secured congressional approval to bridge the Missouri in the nick of time. There remained one final hurdle – the Missouri itself. City of the Future tells us: "The Missouri had never been bridged.... Doubt existed, even among engineers, whether it could be, because of its combination of a powerful current, shifting channel, and disposition to flood. The assignment went to Octave Chanute [shown standing between two associates in picture at left], then chief engineer of the Chicago & Alton....

"Chanute found Kansas City to be equipped with one small foundry and a machine shop. He had to build his own pile-drivers, derricks, and dredges. He had to collect his own data on the behavior of the current from old settlers. After failing twice to place a firm footing under pier 4, he had to import a new technique used on a bridge over the Rhine at Kehl.

"It took Chanute two years and a half, but he bridged the Missouri so successfully that his structure withstood even the great flood of 1903. He was later to be in charge of construction for four railroads...to build the first elevated in New York...and to be elected president of the American Society of Civil Engineers. But he always considered the Kansas City bridge his professional masterpiece."

51

In the Kansas City of 1871, a young man like Wyatt Earp headed for Market Square (left). There he might rub shoulders – and not know it – with Jesse James, who often came into town in disguise. Or he might loll in the shade of stores and saloons, spinning yarns both true and false with colorful characters such as Wild Bill Hickok, Doc Holliday and Bat Masterson. In the book **Wyatt Earp, Frontier Marshal**, Earp tells the way it was:

"During the hot, sunshiny days the men sat around in their shirt-sleeves, with as much pride in fine spotless linen as they had for the velvet-trimmed frock coats and fancy vests which they wore later in the day. Evenings were spent at variety shows, in the dancehalls, or at the theater when a traveling dramatic company was in town. After the show, the real sport of the day got under full steam – monte, faro, and poker. Gambling went on day and night, but the big games rarely started much before midnight.

"There was steady drinking. Kansas City offered a change from the raw liquor of the camps. Saloons were as well stocked with beers, wines, cordials, and fine whiskies as the choosiest drinker could require....

"Conversation dealt with subjects that interested the men, chiefly buffalo-hunting, the rising market for hides, and the increased demand for meat to be shipped East. Conversation not concerned with buffalo, usually dealt with gunplay of another sort, with the sudden end to which some well-known character had come, or a stand against heavy odds by some fighters whom most of the hunters knew. Discussions naturally led to arguments over the merits of weapons and methods of getting them into play. Supporters of any theory were willing and able to demonstrate their points."

Top, left to right: Hickok, Holliday, Masterson, James, and Earp.

Like other major cities, turn-of-the-century Kansas City had its brothels – 147 to be exact. The bon-ton block of sin stretched from Third to Fourth Street on Wyandotte and boasted of swanky, costly houses. The finest, most exclusive and best known was run by Annie Chambers (left). Author W. G. Clugston described the house and its madam: "Her house, with 24 exquisitely furnished rooms, cost $100,000 and was furnished with old masterpieces from Europe. She also possessed other assets and attractions that no competitor could buy or match. She had great beauty, culture and refinement, and her girls were all the cream of the turf, creatures of such allure and charm that more than one successful local businessman chose his wife from among them....

"As she approached the end of her career – when she was nearing 90, and had presided over the same bawdy-house for more than 60 years – Annie became, more than ever, Kansas City's most colorful figure....she wanted to leave a distinctive monument to her memory. She hadn't piled up millions ...but she had her old mansion with its costly furnishings and more than ample means in the bank....

"Annie hit upon the idea of dedicating her remaining years to God and converting her old palace of sin into a shrine of the Saviour. A worker in the City Union Mission had moved into the neighborhood and set up temporary headquarters in a nearby abandoned house. Annie struck up an acquaintance with the man and his wife, and soon was in full partnership with them in their work... she let the missionary move in and set up shop at once, reserving only the right to her old living quarters for herself as long as she lived, and one of the 24 pleasure chambers for one of her lovers as long as he lived...."

A popular place in the 1880s was the intersection of Delaware, Main and Ninth streets – "The Junction." Depicted here by artist James M. Fitzgibbon, "The Junction" almost always bustled with the sounds of a city on the move. People crammed the sidewalks. Horse-drawn carriages battled for the right-of-way. Cable cars clamored down Ninth to Main.

There was a portly man dressed in a conductor's cap, brown vest and green pants, swinging a swagger stick. His name was Mike Tuite, although he was popularly known as "Wide Awake." That was the warning he shouted to pedestrians as the cable car rolled down the hill.

Kansas City has borne its share of insult and eulogy. There were those whose armchair assessments of the country proved shortsighted. And, thankfully, there were those whose rowdy enthusiasm has been vindicated in the twentieth century.

It is not surprising that the change of sentiment from insult to accolade has followed America's course from stuffy provincialism to a robust faith in her manifest destiny. When young America was still scoffing at the Louisiana Purchase, this hostile view of Kansas City greeted readers of **Butler's Geography:** *"This vast region was explored to the headwaters of the Missouri by Lewis and Clark...but such is the dreary and uninviting aspect of the country that no settlements have been made...."*

But such doom-saying was short lived. Explorer John C. Fremont was quick to grasp the opportunity waiting here. *"This is the key to the immense territory west of us,"* he said in 1842.

And no less a man than Senator Thomas Hart Benton had a grand vision of a city cradled in the big bend of the Missouri: *"There...where the rocky bluff meets and turns aside the sweeping current of this mighty river...a large commercial and manufacturing center will congregate, and another generation will see a great city on these hills."*

Twenty years later, in 1873, when much of Benton's vision was realized, William D. Kelley looked to the future of Kansas City: *"I know of no point which opens so wide a market for tomorrow and the next day, and probably the next century."*

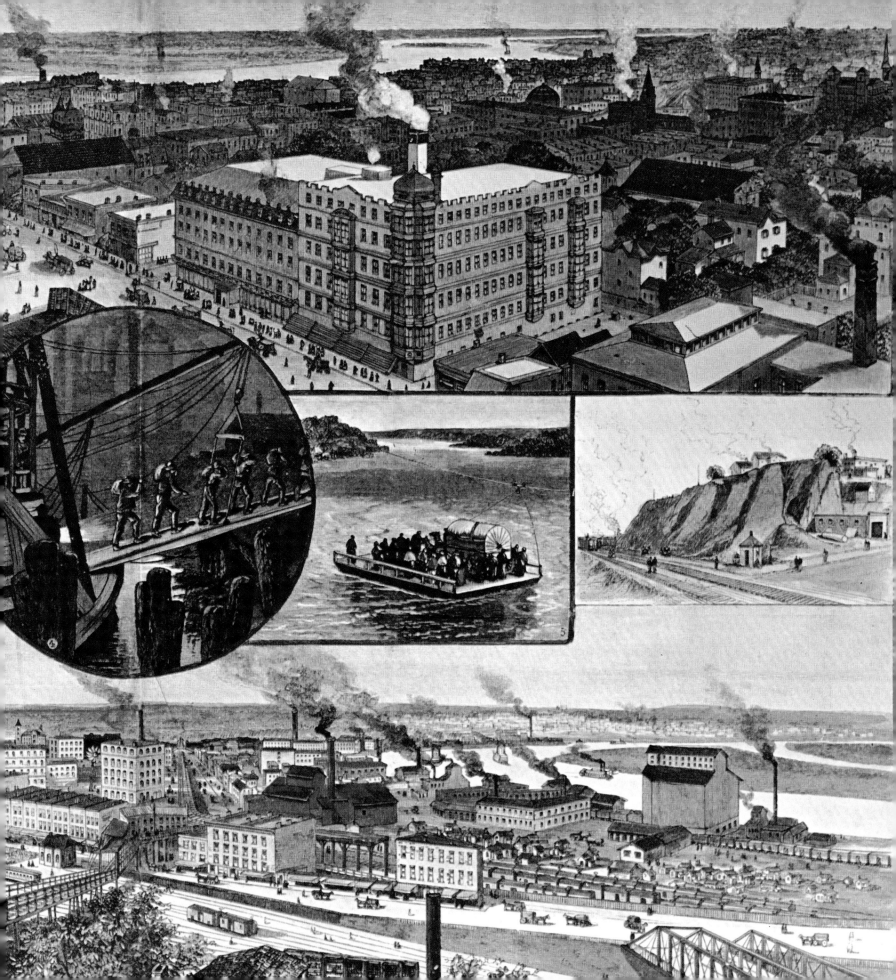

The Movers
and the Makers

Restless. Idealistic. Determined. Strong. These are the words that immediately cross your mind when you try to characterize the kind of men who push back frontiers and carve settlements out of the wilderness. And then, as you think about it further, another word seems more and more to fit with — or maybe even to supersede — all the rest: *audacious*.

Kansas City had taken on the frontier. And by the opening of the twentieth century, this brash city of 163,000 people appeared ready to take on the rest of civilization as well.

They rested their hopes on their new Convention Hall, which had been dedicated in February 1899 with the attending pomp of a John Philip Sousa concert, and which since its opening had hosted a bombastic bill of fare that ranged from grand opera to revival meetings to Epperson's Megaphone Minstrels to the Six-Day Bicycle Races.

But the Show of Shows was to take place on July 4, 1900. These jostling, rough-edged men from this still-green midwestern cow town had had the *audacity* to vie with such established cities as Chicago, Cincinnati, and Milwaukee for one of the biggest events in the country, the Democratic National Convention. Again the unified front, coupled with the traditional Van Horn brand of civic boosterism, had enabled Kansas City to win out over stiff competition.

Yet while city fathers were still gloating over their latest *coup*, their best-laid plans began to go up in smoke. At 1:30 on the afternoon of Wednesday, April 4, 1900, the Kansas City Fire Department had arrived at Thirteenth and Central, along with a crowd of unbelieving onlookers, to find the Convention Hall blazing with a fire so hot it melted glass windows and twisted steel girders into glowing, molten pretzels.

Before the embers had cooled, a group of business and civic leaders had held a meeting and had arrived at an incredible decision: Kansas City wasn't going to stand by while the Democrats shook their heads and packed for Chicago. Kansas City was going to rebuild the Convention Hall in ninety days and hold the convention as planned.

Again, the *audacity*. But they did it. They hired the architect who had designed the now smoldering hall to design a new one. They worked quick arrangements with Pittsburgh's Carnegie Iron Works to supply the steel and with the Minneapolis-based Gilette-Herzog firm to erect the trusses. They launched a city-wide fund drive which netted sixty thousand dollars toward the cost of a new building. They nimbly averted strikes; smoothed over ruffled, deadline-stressed feelings; and even managed to keep chins and progress up despite some particularly unrelenting spring weather.

On July 4, 1900, Democrats from all over the country poured into the flag-draped Kansas City Convention Hall to watch William Jennings Bryan receive the presidential nomination. But

61

Three times Kansas City has invited the politicians to town to conduct business. At the turn of the century, the Democrats elected William Jennings Bryan in the barely completed Convention Hall. In the heyday of "Tom's Town," the austere Herbert Hoover was nominated by the 1928 Republican Convention. In the Bicentennial summer of 1976, the GOP returned to Kansas City. Once again a new hall, the stark-white, twenty-first century coliseum, Kemper Arena, awaited the battle of political wills. President Gerald Ford and his vice-presidential running mate from Kansas, Senator Robert Dole won the nomination but lost the election. As in 1900, Kansas City emerged the real winner.

"The fact is that Kansas City is no longer the rip roarin' Sodom and Gommorah of the Short Grass. It has culture."
— John N. Reddin, Milwaukee Journal

"They are nice people. They are friendly and open, these Kansas Citians. They are the kind who expect that if you're nice to people, they'll be nice back to you. No, they're not naive. They're not unsophisticated, they simply have a different outlook on things from that of some of the cynics who have invaded the city in the past two weeks."
— Sally Quinn, Washington Post

"...if the delegates here were as concerned as they ought to be about our big, ugly, decaying cities, they would look about them at their host, Kansas City. It alone of the cities I know has taken a decisive step to revitalizing city life....But unfortunately, at the convention, with majestic irrelevance, they prefer debating Panama."
— Howard K. Smith, ABC Evening News

Meanwhile, Kansas Citians were reacting to the political ruckus. Said a longtime Democrat-about-town: "Don't matter if they're Republicans, we'll give them a good time. As long as it's only for a week or so, Harry's town and the GOP will get along just fine."

And in the heart of the stockyards, an old-timer was saying, "We've seen action down here — 40,000 head a day and Wyatt Earp, too...and we'll be able to take care of your politicians all right."

the real attraction was the building itself, which was to stand for another thirty-five years and which, from its debut to its demise, loomed in the minds of the citizens who built it as a symbol of something they proudly called "The Kansas City Spirit."

Even today, in an age a little less inclined to blatant boosterism, Kansas Citians seldom get bored hearing the story of the Convention Hall fire. To them, the story capsulizes the kind of drive and unbending dedication that has made this town what it is today. To them, Kansas City Spirit is a basic legacy passed down through generations of forebears — from those who dared to face and settle the frontier, to those who sought out and brought home the railroad, to those who ramrodded the triumph of the Convention Hall trial by fire, to those who today seek to push back the frontiers of international commerce.

It's a toughness, a determination, a civic will nurtured by pride and cultivated by controversy or challenge. Sometimes it comes across as a kind of corn-fed *chutzpah*: "In Kansas City," boasted one businessman at the time of the Convention Hall fire, "we don't know what 'impossible' means."

Kansas City is fortunate to have had at least a handful of leaders to whom nothing seemed impossible — leaders whose dreams didn't get mired in the mud of small river settlements, whose vision was wider than the moment, whose sensibilities were insulted by anything short of the absolute best.

Henry J. Haskell wrote that two things made Kansas City — "the Great Bend of the Missouri and Nelson of the *Star*." When William Rockhill Nelson came to Kansas City from Indiana in 1880, Kansas City insulted his sensibilities. The city lacked paved streets and sidewalks, not to mention the other rudiments of civic polish that Nelson considered basic to the growth of any city. He established the *Kansas City Evening Star*, the town's first afternoon newspaper, and promptly set about to change Kansas City's destiny. Soon he was publishing editorials like this: "Individuals

profit by judicious and liberal expenditures of money. So do cities. Kansas City has reached a point where she must make expenditures if she is to occupy the proud position within her reach. The pinching economy, the picayunish policy, the miserable parsimony, which characterizes our city government must now be abandoned or the city's growth will be seriously retarded and her best interest greatly crippled.

"Kansas City needs good streets, better streetlights, fire protection, a more efficient police force, and many other things which are necessary to the health, prosperity, and growth of a great city. She needs these improvements now. They will cost money, and a great deal of it...."

Obviously, Nelson wasn't interested in mincing words. And he wasn't interested in taking no for an answer, either. He once called the *Star* the *Daily W.R. Nelson*. "People say there are two sides to everything," he used to tell his employees, "but there's only one side — that's our side."

Nelson's side was usually in the best interest of the city, but his civic medicine wasn't always swallowed with gusto. After all, he was dealing with a community molded out of Missouri River clay, and some of the townspeople seemed content to let the clay stay stuck to their boots. But Nelson was going to lift this city out of the mud or know the reason why: he wasn't just a *city father*; he was a *city mother* as well. And Henry J. Haskell has suggested that if the property-owning class had ever put into writing their initial reaction to Nelson's nagging insistence on excellence, it might have gone like this:

"Under the malign direction of Nelson, the *Star* has kept things constantly stirred up. It has made tenants dissatisfied. They never used to complain about light and air. Now they won't look at a house unless every window opens on a flower garden with a hummingbird in it. The *Star* won't let anybody alone. It insists on regulating the minutest detail of people's lives. Its regulations are pernicious and extravagant. Its preaching

William Rockhill Nelson (right, and in Texas-sized hat far right) was a mountain of a man who made The Kansas City Star *(below) and, in turn, Kansas City. Nelson the editor is described by another great editor, William Allen White: "For years thousands of people in Kansas City did refer to him as 'Bill' Nelson, but no one called him 'Bill.' Sooner would one address a heroic statue of Buddha as 'Bud'....The town had to do something with his name; so...he became 'Colonel.' Not that he was ever a colonel of anything: he was just coloneliferous....*

"Through his entire career Mr. Nelson cultivated a sort of elaborate anonymity....'An editor,' he declared, 'should be a kind of political monk; he must take a monastic vow against holding office. For if he doesn't — as sure as God made little apples — they'll get him....'

"Mr. Nelson thought he was not a writer. He never put his pencil to paper. He called one of his editors or reporters...talked the matter in hand over, and the article...appeared to run through the mental machinery of the writer....Often no phrase of his was preserved in articles that pioneered out into new and daring policies....

"...to the millions who came to know and follow the 'Star,' the man who made it great...lived and died a stranger to them. If they met the ruddy-faced, square-shouldered, great-bodied, short-legged, bronze-featured man in the street...doubtless they would turn their heads and say: 'There goes some one!' But only a few... would have identified him with the upstanding, enterprising, wholesome, good-natured newspaper that brought them daily much of their mental and moral and spiritual pabulum."

A new era began early in 1977 when the employee-owned Star was sold to Capitol Cities Communication, Inc. for $125 million, the largest sum ever paid for a single newspaper.

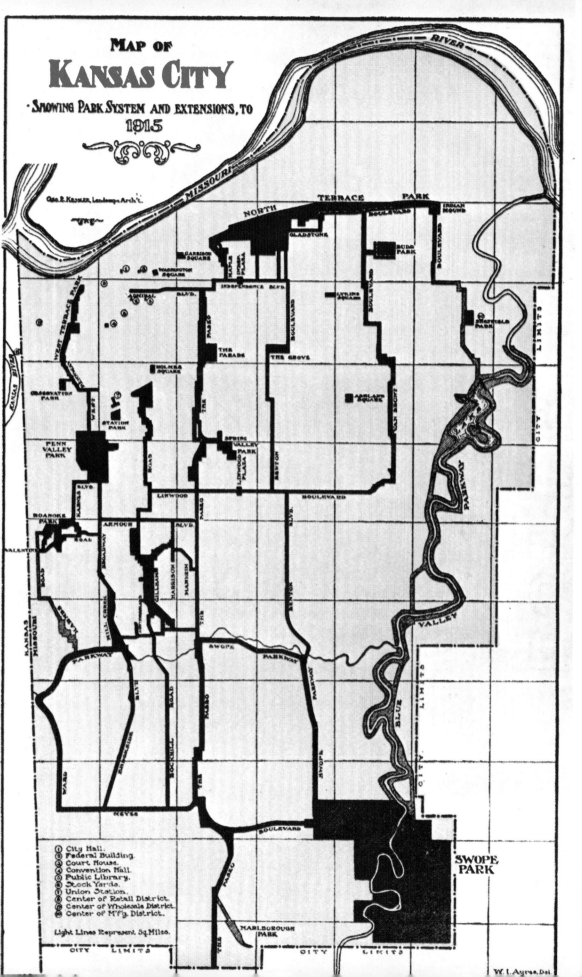

MAP OF
KANSAS CITY
SHOWING PARK SYSTEM AND EXTENSIONS, TO
1915

Geo. E. Kessler, Landscape Arch't.

MISSOURI RIVER

NORTH TERRACE PARK

① City Hall.
② Federal Building.
③ Court House.
④ Convention Hall.
⑤ Public Library.
⑥ Stock Yards.
⑦ Union Station.
⑧ Center of Retail District.
⑨ Center of Wholesale District.
⑩ Center of M'f'g District.

Light Lines Represent Sq. Miles.

SWOPE PARK

W. I. Ayres, Del.

Kansas City's unique boulevard system is a legacy from that nineteenth-century generation of movers and doers like William Rockhill Nelson, A. R. Meyer, George E. Kessler, Kersey Coates, Robert Gillham, Adriance Van Brunt and S. B. Armour. Most of these men gave their names to the belt lines which link points of the city. All of them gave their time, energy and considerable resources.

The plan for an interconnecting system of major boulevards was first promoted by William Rockhill Nelson, who for fifteen years crusaded for an intelligent and generous highway program in the face of opposition from small-minded lovers of the status quo. Eventually, Nelson secured a charter amendment permitting the city to acquire land for the boulevards. The expense of this improvement was to be borne by those properties benefitting, and most property fronting the boulevards reaped an appreciation of from 45 to 500 percent.

Together, Nelson, A. R. Meyer, president of the park board, and George Kessler, landscape architect, mapped out the system. On the north bluffs, where Kersey Coates and his bride had first looked out over the city years before, they carved the beautiful Cliff Drive. From there they planned a belt line circling the city, all the way south to Swope Park and back. Valleys within the city contributed feeders for this trunk system. Almost every major park and neighborhood was interconnected in a system of remarkable style and efficiency.

The boulevard men – clockwise, from upper left: George Kessler, Robert Gillham, Thomas Swope, James Reed, A. R. Meyer, and William Volker. The map (far left) was the plan followed for the Kansas City boulevard system.

about more parks and boulevards and breathing spaces and supervised playgrounds for children, and plant Dorothy Perkins roses, and swat the fly, and housing reform, and a new charter, and art galleries, and keep your lawn trimmed, and take a lot of baths, and throw out the bosses, and use the river, and cut the weeds on vacant lots, and read the Home University Library, and for God's sake don't build such ugly houses, and make the landlord cut a window in the bathroom, and put goats in Swope Park, and why will mothers risk babies' lives by bringing them up on bottles, and plant your bulbs now, and teach your children manners, and what's the use of lawyers, and cultivate a pleasant speaking voice, and build a civic center, and put out houses for the birds, and walk two miles before breakfast, and why are Pullman cars so hot in winter, and go to church, and cut out the children's adenoids, and build trafficways, and sleep with your windows open, and the square deal, and build cyclone-proof houses, and smash the saloons, and pooh, pooh on factories that employ women, and reduce streetcar fares, and go look at Old Masters every Sunday, and use two-by-sixes instead of two-by-fours if you want your house to stand up, and move out in the suburbs, and tear down the tin bridges and build hard surface roads everywhere, and all the other things, has increased the cost of living and given people inflated ideas, and pretty nearly ruined the town."

The classic struggle between the city-as-an-economic-base faction and the city-as-a-place-to-live faction began in 1881 when the *Star* pointed out that, despite Kansas City's growing population, no plans for public recreation had been advanced.

Specifically, this meant parks.

Parks! chortled the opponents, the "moss-backs," as Nelson called them; parks are places where "scented dudes smoke cigarettes and play croquet with girls as silly as themselves."

But Nelson gained steam. Soon he was preaching a boulevard system too. With his own

Today Kansas City has more boulevard miles than Paris. Motorists make their way down 140 miles of broad, expansive thoroughfares and tree-lined parkways. There is an air about these stately and generous boulevards that recalls a long-ago era of gracious living. Unlike the cramped and Gothic avenues of some eastern cities, the broad expanses and beautifully landscaped thoroughfares here seem to reflect the easygoing charm of the Midwest.

Henry J. Haskell has seen the boulevard system as a continuing bulwark of character in the community. He writes: "The boulevards thus helped to zone the city, to prevent the establishing of slum districts, to provide ample areas for low price homes, to create attractive vistas, and to furnish water grade thoroughfares of enormous importance with the growth of motor traffic."

Not the least of the contributions of the boulevard system has been that of bringing picturesque park areas into the very heart of the city. Kansas City seems assured of avoiding the "concrete jungle" stereotype of modern metropolitan centers.

Parts of the original boulevard system are seen on these pages: the grand Paseo, north from 15th Street in 1900 (top left); the Pool Grove at 15th and Benton Boulevard in 1914 (bottom left); the turn at Paseo and 12th Street in 1903 (top right); and Paseo at 18th Street (bottom right).

money he hired a city planner, George Kessler, to sketch out a boulevard plan. Then he enlisted the aid of powerful supporters — the aging visionary from an earlier era, Kersey Coates; Robert Gillham; Adriance Van Brunt; S. B. Armour; and, most valuably, A. R. Meyer, a wealthy industrialist and nature lover whose vision approached the grandiose plane of Nelson's.

Together this group prepared a park and boulevard plan that took almost fourteen years to pass, but which, when it did, established Kansas City as a place sophisticated beyond its time.

Ironically, two men who at first went on record as opposing the park and boulevard system have gone down in local history as having done as much as anyone to make the system a beautiful reality. James Reed, who later became a United States Senator, was elected mayor of Kansas City in 1900. Reed had fought with Nelson and had been accused by the *Star* of trying to wreck the park plans. But the park and boulevard system blossomed as never before during Reed's four years as mayor.

A much less public man, the wealthy, dyspeptic Col. Thomas H. Swope initially opposed the park and boulevard plan because of its inherent threat of higher taxes. But, for whatever reason, Swope had a change of heart. In 1896 he bought and donated to the city a 1,334-acre tract of land four miles out of town specifically earmarked for use as a city park.

Although appreciative, many citizens at the time felt that Swope Park was simply too far out to do the town any good. This so disturbed Col. Swope that he began to brood incessantly. Relatives are said to have heard him often muttering to himself "too far out, too far out."

By 1910 Kansas City had several boulevards completed, others well under way, and could claim 2,118 acres of parks — more than any other American city of comparable size.

Nelson was just one, though perhaps the greatest, of the movers and makers who left their marks on Kansas City.

He was a hard-drinking, farseeing man, was Colonel Tom Swope. He was retiring and shy, a man of few friends. But in 1896 he showed himself to be a true friend of the city by donating 1,334 acres toward the building of a public park. The proposed park was four miles from the city limits. There were those who sneered at the colonel's project, and according to Darrell Garwood, author of Crossroads of America, *scotching the idea that Swope Park was "far out" became the colonel's obsession: "He grew more optimistic about the city's future than he had ever been....He was a slender man, bald except for a fringe, with wide-set eyes that gave him a somewhat child-like appearance despite the mustache he wore. Leaning with one arm on a bar, he would say: 'Young man, has it ever occurred to you that the cities of the Old World grew to a half million before the days of the railroads? Kansas City is in the center of the richest agricultural section of the United States. I won't see it, but you will live to see more than a million people here; perhaps two million. Believe me, Swope Park is none too far out.' "*

Colonel Swope would be gratified to see how "in" his park is today. It boasts two eighteen-hole golf courses. Starlight Theater, one of the most successful outdoor theaters in the United States, lures thousands of Kansas Citians on warm summer evenings to top Broadway and Hollywood productions. The Kansas City Zoo, part of the city scene since 1909, covers about sixty acres of Swope Park and is considered the leading mid-sized zoo in America. Some 600 animals may be seen, including not only the usual elephants, lions, bears, and monkeys but also such creatures as a pygmy marmoset, Bruijn's pademelon, red kangaroo, Masai giraffe, and lesser pandas. The specially designed African veldt area and a large children's zoo section are among the outstanding features that attract some 600,000 persons each year.

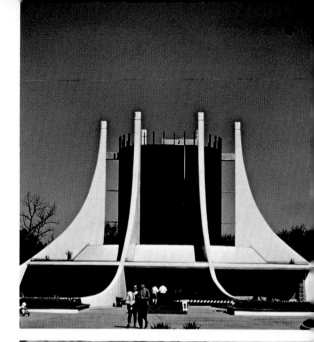

In 1907 J. C. Nichols bought ten acres of land south of Kansas City, and from that sprawling wasteland of hog pastures, slaughter pens, rubbish dumps and stone quarries, he built what is today regarded as one of the most beautiful areas in Kansas City — the Country Club District.

Nichols, like Nelson — and like J. C. Hall, another farsighted Kansas Citian who at about this time had come from Nebraska to establish what would one day be the world's most respected greeting card company — attained his own wealth by pursuing more than money: *quality* was his goal.

In building his homes, Nichols made sure that every house would be a place where people could enjoy *living*. He located the homes on wooded, hilly lots, and instead of straight, sterile, ninety-degree intersections, he built winding roads that met at interesting, intriguing angles. At these intersections he placed art objects — statues, sundials, vases, fountains.

Then, after a six-week trip to Spain, Nichols returned to Kansas City with the vision that was to make him famous: he would build a Spanish-style shopping plaza with scores of intricate discovery shops, the entire area decorated with Spanish tile and fountains and towers; and he would plop this idealized replica of Old Spain smack-dab in the middle of the American Dream — in Kansas City, Missouri, right next to his Country Club residential district.

The Country Club Plaza became the first shopping center in the nation and a source of pride and enjoyment for Kansas Citians.

Nichols knew it would be. His attention to the "frills" of harmony and beauty in city building was rooted in his own refined sensibility; but it also coincided with a basic business insight that apparently escaped his more rawboned contemporaries: "We planned and built this whole District primarily for women and children," he told a *Ladies' Home Journal* writer in 1921. "Women are the home buyers and builders and makers. A man selects a home to please his wife, and women are

Those who knew Jesse Clyde Nichols (right, looking out over his ingenious brainstorm, the Country Club Plaza) remember him as a neighborly, congenial man with a world of welcome in his resonant voice. Yet "neighborly" falls short of describing that part of his nature that was pure, boundless energy. He started to work at age 8, opened his first business at 17, and earned degrees at both Harvard and the University of Kansas. Always he dreamed big dreams. And he was blessed with the practical genius to bring his dreams to fruition.

When he came, Kansas City was only a generation removed from the frontier. Clearly there was something visionary in Nichols's intention to build here a community of beauty and character. Indeed, some who looked upon the acres of hog pasture and rubbish Nichols had purchased beyond city limits branded his dream "idealistic extravagance." But name-calling did not deter this man of unlimited enthusiasm who raised on this wasteland one of the finest and most beautiful developments in the United States. In the Country Club Plaza, it boasts the nation's first shopping center. Its Spanish architecture is appropriately symbolic for a city that once was the head of the Sante Fe Trail. Statuary and sculpture grace the boulevards and parkways. Nichols lavished over $1 million in art objects on the area, but this was part of his dream. He was fond of saying: "A successful real estate man is a trustee of community beauty and loveliness. His job is...to make cities and homes and business centers more lovely and livable."

72

It was built on impulse, and when the heroic bulk of the Liberty Memorial rose in tribute to Kansas City's fighting sons, men knew the impulse had been a good one. Even before the signing of the armistice in 1918, the city was seized by a spontaneous urge to commemorate the sacrifice and striving of the great war. Less than three weeks after cease-fire, the city council called a mass meeting and the Liberty Memorial project was under way, as described in City of the Future: "No money raising campaign in Kansas City to that time had ever been so ambitious or so thoroughly planned. It was a drive for 2 million dollars for the memorial linked with the regular charities campaign for $500,000. Saturday before the opening of the campaign Kansas City paraded. The line of school children marching twelve abreast was four blocks long, only one of the parade features....

"Selecting the design for the memorial enlisted the top architectural talent of the United States. The judges finally were unanimous in the choice of the design submitted by H. Van Buren Magonigle of New York.

"...The official dedication of the memorial...was another great day in Kansas City. Armistice Day, 1926, President Calvin Coolidge spoke to a throng probably greater than the one that had greeted the allied commanders five years before....

"The recklessly ambitious Liberty Memorial movement characterized Kansas City in its rambunctious 1920s. At no time in the city's history had its leadership been more confident of manifest destiny."

On November 1, 1921, the allied military leaders of World War I gathered in Kansas City for the dedication of the Liberty Memorial site (bottom right). Left and top right are two views of the Liberty Memorial today.

more sentimental and artistic than men. Things of beauty appeal more strongly to women. We know that if we can have the women of this District love it and be proud of it as their home neighborhood, its future will be assured."

Kansas City has traditionally made its most dramatic progress through the efforts and actions of its farsighted private citizens — from Coates and Van Horn in the early years, to Nelson and Nichols in this century. And in between, a procession of leaders and doers had marched across the cityscape with varying degrees of civic impact: Robert Gillham and his cable railway; R.A. Long and the Liberty Memorial; Arthur Stilwell and his railroad; William Volker and his parole board. Coates and Van Horn played a big part in *taming* the frontier. Nelson and Nichols and the rest did much to *civilize* it.

One of the ironies of life seems to be that as the great, individual leaders set in motion their expansive schemes to bring about civilization, they at the same time ensure the extinction of themselves as a species. Civilization brings systems; systems bring red tape; red tape locks us into an interdependence that clips the wings of the freewheeling one-man show. Today even a Nelson couldn't get a convention hall built in ninety days.

But civilization just limits the mobility, it doesn't kill the spirit. Colorful characters are part of Kansas City's heritage, and there have always been men in this town who in themselves reflect the tone of their particular age: the swaggering Wyatt Earp and the boy-faced killer Jesse James in the lawless 1870s; the hard-nosed Nelson in the turn-of-the-century years of unlimited destiny; and the domineering Tom Pendergast in the corrupt 1920s and 1930s.

Pendergast is the stuff fiction is made of. As head of a far-reaching, well-oiled political machine that derived huge sums from gambling and prostitution, Pendergast wielded such power that citizens wryly referred to his tiny office at 1908 Main Street as the capitol of Missouri.

Perhaps the most beneficial thing Pendergast ever did for Kansas City was to help Harry Truman take his first step to the White House. When Truman decided to get out of his haberdashery business and run for the post of county judge, the Pendergast machine backed him all the way. Boss Tom reportedly passed along two bits of advice to the young politician: "Keep your word when you give it"; and, "When you're after votes, don't wear two-toned shoes, and be sure to wear a coat and pants that match."

Pendergast reigned supreme in Kansas City for thirteen years, and during that time he and his puppet city manager, Henry F. McElroy, bilked the town for all they could get. Pendergast himself owned the Ready-Mixed Concrete Company, and during the thirties the saying was that Pendergast lieutenants "examined everything they saw, and if it didn't move they poured concrete on it." In J. C. Nichols's Country Club Plaza, for example, the tiny stream of water known as Brush Creek today runs along a concrete bed more than two miles long, seventy feet wide, eight inches thick — thanks to Tom Pendergast.

In 1936 the *Kansas City Star* — under the leadership of then managing editor Roy Roberts (a mover in his own right) — launched a massive voting fraud investigation which eventually opened the closet doors of city hall and bared the skeletons crammed inside. In 1939 Pendergast went to prison for income tax evasion. Five years later he was dead.

But while he lived, Boss Tom Pendergast at least provided another dimension to that legacy of Kansas City Spirit that has marked Kansas City's most influential movers and makers through the years. Unfortunately, Pendergast's spirit was drawn from a well of corruption, while Nelson's — and that of others like him — was drawn from a purer well of civic and personal pride.

One writer has lamented the fact that William R. Nelson died before Tom Pendergast reached his full power. "That," says the writer, "would have been a collision of buffalo."

The smiling faces, the marcelled pompadours, and happy poses seen here give us a charming glimpse of an utterly vanished yesterday. Gone are the days of all-night jam sessions, the dueling saxophonists, and red-hot mamas. But while they lasted, the halcyon days of jazz meant something special to Kansas City. It was here that an eleven-year-old boy named Euday Bowman wrote the famous "Twelfth Street Rag," immortalizing the Kansas City thoroughfare where they first danced the Charleston to the driving beat of jazz.

There were perhaps fifty clubs in the Twelfth Street area. Each was redolent with smoke, choked with patrons consuming bootleg spirits, crawdads, ribs, and chili, then rocking to the lubricious sounds of boogie-woogie. Here jazz great Charlie "Yardbird" Parker (right) learned to blow the big blues sound. Count Basie (far right) formed the Kansas City Seven at the local Reno Club and pioneered that hearty and corn-fed music known as "Kansas City blues." Other artists like Hot Lips Page, Bennie Moten and his orchestra (top left), the Albert Williams-Christina Buckner group (right), and comic Red Skelton got their start in K.C.'s tenderloin district. "In those days," said Count Basie, "when they opened a club they took the key to the door and handed it with a five dollar bill to a cab driver and told him, 'Ride as far as that'll take you, then throw the key away.'"

One of the reasons clubs never closed was stars like Julia Lee. Performing in brother George's band (bottom left), she sang her way to stardom and a command performance for Harry Truman at the White House. She was famous for hot songs like "Snatch 'n' Grab It" and her special rapport with fans. Author Carey Tate recalls, "For years Midwesterners have admired Julia Lee for being a jolly mother confessor to the depressed spirits of her audiences. She usually ends a song with an invitation, 'Let's sit down 'n' drink it over.'"

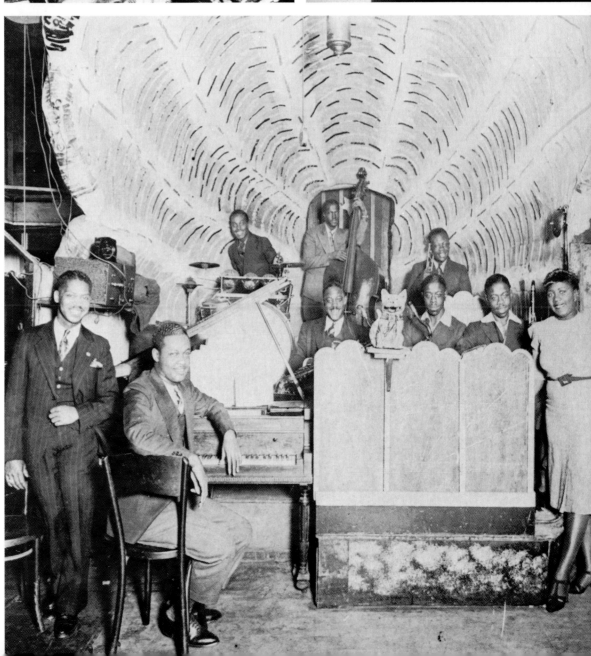

Kansas City has seen a heap of living in its time. There have been substantial changes since it was the outpost of the "Great American Desert." Yesterday's bullwhacking, feverish town of Westport is now a lively shopping district of boutiques, flea markets, galleries, and specialty shops for leather, pottery, fabrics and imports. Ironically, yesterday's Wiedenmann Brothers grocery store is today's Kelly's tavern (lower right).

Vinegar Hill has become the lovely Penn Valley Park. And next door, the ugly old eyesore of Signboard Hill has been transformed into the gracious mid-city complex of Crown Center (right center). Here, too, offices, apartments, restaurants, and total living facilities make the area seem a thousand years removed from its derelict past.

But Kansas City reveres the things of the past that are sound and good. There is no indiscriminate destruction accompanying its urban renewal. Downtown, the New York Life Building (upper right), first of the city's skyscrapers, stands as mute witness to the realized dreams of the founding fathers. A remarkable building in its own right, built entirely without structural steel, this McKim, Meade, and White creation stretches to the maximum height possible for masonry walls. It is capped with a two-ton bronze eagle, cast in one piece by Louis Saint-Gaudens and mounted in 1891.

Southeast of this landmark is little old St. Mary's Church (left). More modest in concept than her skyscraper neighbor, she nevertheless symbolizes the harmony of past and present in Kansas City. Her crotchety red bulk is right at home with the concrete sweep of the Federal Building across the street. As a local architect reflected, "Nothing's quite so exciting as the new with a bit of the old left in."

From the time of the Irish potato famine to the Vietnamese war, America's cities have offered the best hope for a better life to millions of immigrants. Work in the packinghouses or on the railroad drew many of Kansas City's ethnic groups, and most settled first in the North End or the West Bottoms.

The Irish came early to cut streets through the bluffs and to make bricks for those streets. They stayed to use their gifts of language and wit in politics and parishes.

The blacks came as slaves and stayed as free men. Today Kansas City's 112,000 blacks are shifting geographical and occupational boundaries. They gave Kansas City jazz and barbecue. Now they're also producing doctors and politicians.

"Little Italy," the colorful section between downtown and the river known as the "North End," was settled from 1890 to 1920. Some forty thousand Kansas Citians today can claim a parent or grandparent born in Italy.

Jobs on the Santa Fe brought the Mexican-Americans between 1910-1920. Language, tradition, and religion give them a strong sense of community on the West Side and in the Argentine district.

Of many differing nationality backgrounds, Kansas City's Jewish community finds great strength in collective action through diverse organizations, such as the Jewish Community Center and Hebrew Academy and exerts influence far beyond their numbers in the arts, professions, and civic leadership.

While only Italians, Mexican-Americans, and blacks still live in geographically defined areas on the Missouri side, over in Kansas City, Kansas, a roll call of churches is a roster of ethnic neighborhoods: St. Joseph's, Polish; St. George's, Serbian Orthodox; Holy Trinity, Russian Orthodox; St. Cyril's, Slovak; St. Anthony's, German; Holy Family, Slovene, to name a few. Up on Strawberry Hill Croatian families work together to preserve ethnic music and dance in the annual spring Tamburitzan Festival.

Kansas Citians revel in the cuisines, fetes, and traditions of many ethnic groups. Former Mayor Ilus Davis has long maintained that the ethnic mix in Kansas City closely parallels the national percentages. Ethnically speaking, as Kansas City goes, so goes the country!

That Kansas City Style

"...a cracker town, but a happy town."

— Count Basie

Down in Kansas City's central business district, they have erected significant spires — not all at once, but orderly and beautifully. Some are old friends, like the early thirties Art Deco Kansas City Power and Light Building and City Hall, the tallest city hall in the country. In the financial district, the contemporary Commerce Towers and TenMain Center, Harry Weese's bank building, and City Center Square are architectural odes to the miracles of concrete and steel, glass and chrome. Each spire, old or new, familiar or startling, adds its unique texture, creating a visually satisfying monument to tomorrow.

Over west on Eleventh Street stands a monument of considerably more regional and historic substance: an enormous brown-and-white-painted Hereford bull perched majestically above the city on a 101-foot pedestal.

Somewhere between those two monuments lies the heart — the spiritual heart — of Kansas City. This has always been a city of contradictions. It wasn't supposed to survive its rustic infancy, but it did. It wasn't supposed to land the railroad, but it did. It wasn't supposed to rebuild the Convention Hall in time for the 1900 Democratic Convention, but it did. It wasn't supposed to re-emerge after devastating floods in 1903, 1951, and 1977, but it did. It wasn't supposed to snap back from the shattering, demoralizing experience of the Pendergast era, but it did. And more recently, it wasn't supposed to survive crippling construction strikes in 1969-70, but it did.

Yet today, some 150 years after the fact, the Great American Desert Theory still taints the Kansas City image along both American coasts: Kansas City is supposed to be built on a flat, desolate prairie, but it's not. It's supposed to be a cultural wasteland, but it's not. It's supposed to be peopled by simple, sauntering, rawboned dirt farmers and raucous rivermen. It's not.

This is a city: eclectic, electric, an urbane organism that grew out of the heartland's mind and spirit, satisfying its common needs and crystallizing its fondest dreams. This is a city, and it does what cities are supposed to do.

Today glinting skyscrapers sprout where once was golden wheat. Expressways wind about the countryside, paving cow paths and wagon trails. Jets swoop low over rolling Missouri farmland to land at one of the world's most modern airports. A unique inland foreign trade zone provides the impetus for Kansas City to push back the frontiers of international commerce. She does her pioneering in medical labs, in inner city development, in city college systems, in all-encompassing transportation facilities. And she asserts, proves, reaffirms her refined cosmopolitan tastes by oohing and aahing at Colonel Nelson's art gallery; by donating money to the flowering of an orchestra, a lyric opera, a repertory; by attending glittering balls on their behalf. This is a *city*. Though it started as farmland, it's been a long time since Kansas City was just a part of Gabriel Prudhomme's south forty.

Yes. But that's not to say that Prudhomme's south forty isn't still a big part of Kansas City. Which brings you back to the original question of Kansas City's heart. The image builders — the twentieth-century Van Horns — will try to convince you that what's keeping this city alive is a tremendous stainless steel heart just pumping for progress.

There are others, though, who will tell you it's not so. That Kansas City's heart is deeply rooted in things more earthy and elemental than stainless steel; not only in Herefords and farmlands per se, but in the ideas they convey — fresh air and open spaces; rural honesty and independence; hard work and play; clean, simple living; and a reverence and respect for the good, basic things in life: friendship, laughter, heritage, and the pursuit of personal happiness.

Kansas City "Style" was first a musical term referring to that classic blend of blues and ragtime that came to identify and explain Kansas City to millions of jazz buffs.

Jazz. The very word is sensuous, and in the twenties and thirties, jazz was a way of life in Kansas City. "It was a town of sin and sax-ophonists," says one jazz historian. Each element supported the other, and it was all nestled snugly into the cozy permissiveness fostered by Boss Tom Pendergast.

As the sun set over the stockyards, herds of people would begin to prowl along Kansas City's Twelfth Street, for years one of America's most notorious neon strips. Prohibition was something you read about in the newspaper, and the newspaper was something you used to wrap shells of shrimp and crawfish that most Kansas City clubs offered free in tremendous lard cans to get customers to drink up a little bit more. Chili and short ribs flavored the air up and down Twelfth Street, and it all mixed with the hot, earthy smells wafting up from the stockyards and the packing plants.

In this environment, some of the best jazz in America was blown into many a smoky Twelfth-Street morning: Charlie "Bird" Parker, Mary Lou Williams, Benny Moten, Hot Lips Page, Julia Lee, Baby Lovett — these were but a few of the musicians helping to nurture the Kansas City Style. The music was unrestrained,

and so were the times. Prostitution, gambling, political corruption, dope, gangland murder — all were part of daily living in the Kansas City of the twenties and thirties.

But Pendergast went to prison, and the party ended. It had been fun, exciting, romantic — but no way to build a city.

So the city reformed. Today the Kansas City Style is a far cry from the sin-and-saxophone life-style of before. There's plenty of color left, it's just not as flamboyant. And Kansas City's style is all its own. Not the hurried, grimacing, frazzled existence of New York. Not the hip, finger-snapping abandon of Los Angeles. Not the "my gracious" drawl of New Orleans.

Put it this way. If cities were school kids, New York might pick fights in the parking lot during lunch; Los Angeles might wear psychedelic tank shirts and amber glasses and have a surfboard rack attached to its candy-apple car; New Orleans might wear knit ties and write poetry and pore over William Faulkner and Walker Percy. And Kansas City? Kansas City would go out for football and in the off-season play third-chair cornet in the band. It would have a tough time with algebra and would get its girl to help. And it would take that girl to the prom, corsage and all, and awkwardly but ecstatically dance the new dances while wishing fervently that its new hair style would lie down like it's supposed to.

Kansas City is the red-blooded, all-American city — friendly, well scrubbed, unpretentious, candid, enthusiastic. And yet not without an awareness that in weaker moments breeds uncertainty, even inferiority. Like Colonel Swope with his park, Kansas City sometimes feels the need to prove itself, to convince the world that, Great American Desert bedamned, Kansas City — in terms of culture, business acumen, heritage, livability, and potential — is none too far out. Colonel Swope was vindicated, and so — if the world could visit — would be Kansas City.

From the seed of the tiny fur-trading commu-

The Plaza Art Fair is almost fifty years old and an institution in Kansas City. Its Mardi Gras atmosphere reflects the informal midwestern approach to culture.

Beautiful Indian summer lends itself to the magic of this annually awaited event held outdoors in the midst of the historic Country Club Plaza. Thousands of Kansas Citians are joined by people from all over the Midwest. They come to buy, see, and take part in this gathering of the best of American art.

In one sense, this is a Missouri version of the Baghdad market. Everything is going on at once. There are hot dog vendors and stately continental restaurants nearby. A live string ensemble serenades with chamber music. The omnium-gatherum air is reinforced by the bewildering variety of art wrought in watercolor, oil, acrylic, pen and ink, charcoal, conté crayon, clay, stone, iron, copper, brass, and silver.

The Art Fair provides a unique opportunity for the artist to meet his public. Old friendships are renewed and new friends made every year. Suburbanites rub shoulders with connoisseurs buying for private collections. They're both at home here, for the Fair has something for everyone.

The whole idea is preservation, not demolition, and the idea is working. The Kansas City Landmarks Commission, appointed by City Hall, has joined forces with the Historic Kansas City Foundation, a group of private citizens with money, energy, and influence to save our most historic and architecturally significant old buildings. The effort is paying off.

For example, a handsome Ninth Street block of 1880s vintage from Wyandotte to Baltimore will now remain intact. The Folly Theater, once headed for the wrecking ball, is being restored for an exciting theatrical future. The old Hyde Park residential area, with its jewel, Janssen Place, leads the movement in neighborhood restoration.

In historic Westport outfitters once supplied the needs of wagon trains headed west and saloons the needs of crews for one last fling. Today the moldering, low-rise, brick structures have been dramatically recycled and adapted for contemporary uses – a historic setting for a modern scene. The streets are alive with hip style and vibrant music, the night spots and restaurants jammed on weekends with the young and fun loving. It's a place to browse and buy, to stroll along lantern-lighted streets, or to sit, nibble, and people-watch, perhaps in the popular Jack Straw Courtyard behind the Prospect of Westport.

Historic restoration combines aesthetics with economics. It recognizes the colossal waste in knocking down one building to raise another. It suggests that blending the old and new creates a more interesting, more rare urban fabric than either alone. Architects talk of treating the best of the old as a resource from which to build. The result is a more complex, visually satisfying city.

nity on the Missouri River, this city has grown in all directions. It sprawls over 2,768 square miles of wooded, rolling hills accented by limestone and rock strata where expressways have been cut to connect the ever-widening circle of suburban communities with the city's core.

Downtown Kansas City — like many a downtown across the United States — is mostly a place to work; the city lives in the suburbs. Kansas Citians might well be the models for suburban, middle-class living: their vestigial respect for the land causes them to spend hours, and fortunes, in neighborhood lawn-and-garden stores; they laboriously map out weekend itineraries of garage sales, which they attend in eternal quest of that middle-class grail, The Bargain; they recapture the flavor of their past in the hickory aura of patio cookouts. On the whole, they are joiners — service clubs, garden clubs, country clubs, churches. They are crusaders lending valuable time to Scouts, Indian Guides, Little League, charities.

They are nightclubbers with plenty of watering holes to keep them busy. They are partygoers, dressing up at the drop of a top hat for social events ranging from a "Breath of Spring Ball" to a gathering of outdoor types determined to toast the beginning of duck season.

Kansas Citians are fresh-air freaks — boating, biking, picnicking, backpacking, skiing, camping, golfing. They are premier sports fans and players of everything from Frisbee to football, golf to croquet, bowling to tennis. Since the turn of the century, they've cheered baseball and, later, football teams through season after spotty season — the minor-league baseball Blues, the all-black Monarchs, and the hapless Athletics, snatched away at first promise by the locally infamous Charles O. Finley. In the thirties, the mediocre Kansas City Cowboys rode quickly into the sunset of professional football history.

But the Kansas City fans, as dedicated as they are dapper, and always angry at Howard Cosell,

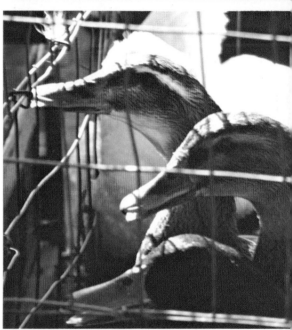

have begun to see their loyal tenacity pay off. They've watched their Royals, the locally-owned baseball team, make it to the league play-offs. They've seen their Chiefs win the Super Bowl. They've cheered the Kings, their basketball team. And in homage to its own favorite pastimes, this town of Kansas City fans has constructed the $64 million Harry S. Truman dual stadium sports complex, the only one of its kind in the country.

Energetic. Outgoing. Uninhibited in their own element. You don't watch long, you participate, and then you begin to understand the Kansas City life-style: action-oriented rather than contemplative; of the body, not necessarily the mind. It's an outdoor culture. Nothing so wicked as classic hedonism — just a healthy, red-blooded, midwestern regard for plunging in and living.

Stainless steel? Yes, and plenty of it, for it's always been a Kansas City tradition to keep up with the times. Capital-C Culture? Yes, that too, for Kansas City certainly appreciates the value of art and beauty.

But at its heart, Kansas City is not tomorrow, nor is its life lived on the airy plane of exquisite sensibilities. Kansas City is today, very much in touch with the past but primarily concerned with the spontaneous needs and joys of living now. Above all, Kansas City is a place for people — because its people have built it that way, tailoring it to their own seemingly uncomplicated sense of what life is all about.

It's been called a cow town and a hick town, and probably worse. Its young intellectuals have chalked it off as hopelessly square.

No apologies are necessary. The critics will come around. Count Basie, who was here during an earlier era of the Kansas City Style, perhaps said it best: "...a cracker town, but a happy town." At this stage in the life of the American city, how can you apologize for one that its people still enjoy?

"There are two great super powers in the world today...Saudi Arabia and Kansas," reflected an Italian news correspondent visiting Kansas City recently. He was watching activity at the Kansas City Board of Trade, the world's largest marketplace for hard red wheat, the nation's key export commodity.

With world food needs rapidly emerging as an urgent concern, Kansas Citians, once embarrassed by their cow-town image, have reassessed their basic ties to agriculture. Kansas City a cow town? No. Agribusiness capital? You bet. For example: In 1978 sales receipts from agribusiness and agricultural products in metropolitan Kansas City totaled over $7 billion. That's the same as moving a company the size of U.S. Steel to town.

Kansas City sprawls in the center of America's most fertile land: Kansas, Missouri, Nebraska, and Iowa. Within six hundred miles of this booming metropolis, 78% of the nation's wheat is grown, 89% of its hogs, 80% of its cattle, 90% of its corn, 93% of its sorghum, and 89% of its soybeans.

Excellent transportation systems exist in all directions; means of commodity exchange and distribution are active. As former Mayor Charles Wheeler wryly commented, "God and geography have been good to us."

91

"The people are the city" wrote William Shakespeare. And in the Country Club Plaza one senses that Kansas City's people are very happy. Here the familiar life rhythms of ordinary people lend music and meaning to the place.

Lovers walk hand in hand. There are little knots of art students sketching buildings, trees, and fountains. Around the next corner there may be a folk guitarist or a whole jazz band. Old friends chat in a sidewalk cafe, leading the life of **boulevardiers**. Smartly dressed women tour the elegant assortment of stores, shops and boutiques. Boys and girls bubble with excitement, finding the Plaza one delightfully frothy hippity-hop from a fabulous pastry shop to a world of ice-cream wonders.

Children have always been important to the Plaza. There are pet shows here. And every Easter a family of big ceramic rabbits delights youngsters on every street corner.

But perhaps the winter holiday season holds the real enchantment. On Thanksgiving evening hundreds of people book hotel rooms overlooking the Plaza. Hundreds more gather in the streets to listen to band music, carollers, and to await the annual lighting of the Plaza. All at once, thousands of lights are lit and the brilliant colors of Christmas outline every building and thoroughfare. There are oohs and ahs, little boys and girls clapping hands, toasts drunk to health and prosperity...and not an unhappy face in sight.

Midway between the Country Club Plaza and downtown is Crown Center, a $500 million, eighty-five-acre "city within a city" developed with private capital and an eye toward public enrichment.

Conceived in the mid-1950's by Joyce C. Hall of Hallmark Cards, Inc., the architectural showplace has been executed by Hall's son, Donald, president of the family-owned greeting card firm.

When completed in 1988, the vast development will add some fifty buildings to the Kansas City skyline, including hotels, office towers, retail complexes, condominiums and apartments, restaurants, pocket parks, and its busy central square.

Completed in 1980 are the Crown Center Hotel and the Hyatt Regency, two major office complexes, the shopping center of ninety stores, and the first residential neighborhood. Edward Larrabee Barnes is the master planner and coordinating architect and buildings have been designed by Harry Weese, The Architects Collaborative, Bruno Conterato, Warren Platner, PBNDML, and Barnes himself.

Just ten blocks from the heart of the central business district, Crown Center has become a popular gathering place for the six-state central plains region. Visitors from throughout the nation enjoy the sixty-foot waterfall of the Crown Center Hotel lobby as it tumbles down a craggy hill that is a verdant jungle of drooping Florida fig trees and buxom hydrangeas.

The soaring atrium at the Hyatt Regency was inspired by the Galleria in Milan and Mark Twain's famous account of relaxing there. Nearby, the sculptures of Alexander Calder and David Smith look over the community activities of the Central Square, be they sack races, ballet, or ice skating.

An idealism is being realized at Crown Center; quality design and the public interest are successfully merged by private resources.

94

The American Royal is the largest combined livestock, horse show and rodeo in the United States. For two weeks every fall it draws 1,700 horses and 4,000 head of prime cattle, sheep, and swine from thirty-five states and Canada. Since 1899 it has been a Kansas City tradition.

Housed in the snow-white, space-age Kemper Arena, the Royal is at once part of the rural past and part of a demanding future for agribusiness. It is an awesome entertainment, a stockmen's jamboree, and workshop for progress and improvement.

As a showcase for livestock, it brings together the best efforts of North American breeders and indicates future trends in the industry. Tradition dictates that, after a convivial auction breakfast, the Kansas City business community bid on blue-ribboned Royal champions and donate them to worthy causes.

Grain, wool, and the latest farm equipment are exhibited, and farmers and processors talk shop. The Belles of the American Royal sponsor the BOTAR Ball which opens the winter social season. But most of the 300,000 people who attend every year come to enjoy the hoopla and excitement of it all. They applaud proud Arabians, Morgans, and Appaloosas; thrill at the high-stepping harness horses; and marvel at the rodeo cowboy's nerve and skill. They meander through rows of lethargic cattle with exotic breed names and mingle with stockmen in Stetsons, aristocratic equestrians, and royal-blue-jacketed, fresh-faced Future Farmers of America.

For fifty years the FFA has held its annual convention in Kansas City in conjunction with the Royal. The presence of these 22,000 farm boys and girls tugs at the urban conscience. They are a reminder of values learned living close to the land.

The Royal is highly youth-oriented. In addition to the FFA, 4-H Club youths are in town showing at the Royal, and collegiate competitors are learning the craft of meat and livestock judging. For equitation riders under eighteen, the Royal represents the coveted ultimate goal – the national finals.

There is something about eating that brings out the expert in everybody. Ask about a good place to eat and you're likely to get a discourse on the greatest, most fantastic restaurant in the world. Kansas City is known for its fine restaurants. For two reasons. One, it is hard to keep your tongue from wagging after biting into a juicy Kansas City steak. Two, humorist Calvin Trillin – born and fed in Kansas City, now a New Yorker – has made a career of trumpeting Kansas City's culinary delights and once wrote for Playboy:

"The best restaurants in the world are, of course, in Kansas City. Not all of them; only the top four or five....

"...the single best restaurant in the world is Arthur Bryant's Barbeque....Bryant's specializes in barbecued spareribs and barbecued beef – the beef sliced from briskets of steer that have been cooked over a hickory fire for thirteen hours. When I'm away from Kansas City and depressed, I try to envision someone walking up to the counterman at Bryant's and ordering a beef sandwich to go – for me."

Not many eaters in Kansas City are depressed these days because uplifting barbecue is available at Gates', Snead's, and Hayward's, as well as Bryant's and other spots. Elsewhere, more and more palates are drifting away – now and then – from the savory sirloin staples that have sustained the community for decades.

Natives of Peking seek out the Princess Garden for a taste of home, but there is also Wu's, The Imperial Palace, Tokyo Plaza, and Hibachi among many Oriental restaurants. Gus Riedi's La Bonne Auberge and the La Mediterranee shun the grill and prepare sauces in the Gallic tradition. Other traditions are the Savoy Grill and the Hereford House. Truly, the culinary alphabet runs from A (The American at Crown Center) to Z (Zarko's homemade sausages and deli in the suburbs).

During the thirties, when notorious political boss Tom Pendergast was calling the shots, Kansas City was a wide-open, hell-bent-for-leather town. One wag jibed, "If you want to see some sin, forget about Paris and go to Kansas City. With the possible exception of such renowned centers as Singapore and Port Said, Kansas City probably has the greatest sin industry in the world."

Kansas City nightlife today is less gaudy and more stylish than in those bawdy days of brothels and bathtub gin. Today, the disco beat vibrates through night spots such as Biba's, while the jazz that became synonymous with Kansas City can be heard in informal jam sessions at the Mutual Musicians Foundation long after the city's working musicians have left their paying jobs – this is jamming at its best.

There is something for everybody. For the briefcase set, there is the gallery of nostalgic signs at Signboard Bar. For those happy in the crush of a crowd, there's the whimsical surroundings of Fred P. Otts, the excitement of Kelly's, or the European flavor of Houlihan's Old Place.

Then there are the dinner theaters. These lively showhouses regularly feature Broadway hits and bright new plays. The nation's critics have recognized that everything is up to date in Kansas City with the simple observation that the city's dinner theaters are "the most successful...in America today."

Visitors to Kansas City's Nelson Gallery of Art delight in the way the building opens onto the baroque columns of Kirkwood Hall and the Roman renaissance charm of the Rozzelle courtyard. But the Nelson belongs to no single period. Its south lawn is the setting for Henry Moore's "Sheep Piece" (facing page). Among its recent acquisitions are Degas' "Les Petites Modistes," Morisot's "La Reveuse," Winslow Homer's "Gloucester Harbor" and Frederic Edwin Church's "Jerusalem from the Mount of Olives." Two important works by Mary Cassatt and Paul Gauguin, and a Baroque portrait by renowned French court painter, Hyacinthe Rigaud, also are recent additions. The scope of seventeenth- and eighteenth-century Italian and French painting is demonstrated in trhee major new masterworks: "Piazza del Popolo, Rome" by Panini, "Holy Family" by Procaccini, and Chardin's "Still Life With Cat and Fish." In less than two years the Nelson has hosted two significant international exhibits: "Archaeological Finds of the People's Republic of China" and "Sacred Circles: 2000 Years of American Indian Art." Both attracted record crowds. Like the city, this is a cosmopolitan museum whose faces include the solemn Flemish look of Petrus Christus's "Madonna and Child in a Gothic Interior" (upper left); the lazy, beguiling quality of "Whiling Away the Summer" (upper right), an unusual ink and color painting on silk from fourteenth-century China; and the sensitivity of the world-famous work by Rembrandt, "Portrait of a Youth With a Black Cap" (center left). "Le Jardin des Mathurins" (center right) by Camille Pissarro is joined by one of the gallery's proudest possessions, "Boulevard des Capucines, Paris" by Claude Monet (lower left). This painting and "The Sacrifice of Abraham" (lower right) by Rubens are among the museum's most popular pieces, those that patrons of all ages pause to linger over and remember.

The William Rockhill Nelson Gallery and Mary Atkins Museum of Fine Arts had its inception at the turn of the century when Nelson and other civic leaders began lobbying for a landmark cultural center in Kansas City.

The project, according to City of the Future, received unexpected impetus in the person of shy, retiring Mary Atkins:

"In the midst of this long struggle, 1911, Mary McAfee Atkins died leaving the $300,000 residue of her estate for the building of a gallery. The news burst on the art-starved city. Few persons had known this strange, spinsterish woman....At home she was penurious and almost a recluse. But in the last years...she found in the great European galleries an inspiration that brought meaning to the civic urge back home."

In 1933 the commanding classic lines of the museum took shape on a twenty-acre tract that had been the homesite of William Nelson. Charles Keck was commissioned to execute four exterior wall murals depicting the conquest of the west in bas-relief. Inside, the great central Kirkwood Hall was finished with twelve towering columns of black marble.

Today the Nelson is the largest museum between Chicago and Tokyo. It is ranked among the nation's half-dozen top museums and houses the elegant, eight-foot sculpture of Kuanyin on a Rockery (right) – part of the gallery's collection of oriental art. That it is perhaps the best such collection outside of Asia is due largely to the genius of the gallery's director emeritus, Laurence Sickman.

The Helen and Kenneth Spencer Art Research Library was dedicated in late 1978, greatly expanding and enriching the Nelson's facilities for art students and historians.

Although Nelson provided that his funds could be used to purchase only those works of artists dead at least thirty years, later bequests have made possible the purchase of modern paintings like pop artist Tom Wesselmann's "Great American Still Life." Wesselmann's work joins that of old masters Titian, Goya, Reynolds, Copley, El Greco, Rembrandt, Rubens, and Van Gogh.

The museum is currently experiencing a vital period of growth, an exciting trend toward an increase in gifts. The diversified interests in the arts of its dynamic director, Ralph T. Coe, are reflected in creative new attitudes and directions.

As the so-called "Heart of America," it is only right that Kansas City is a center for education.

In the Kansas City area, there are ten bachelor and graduate degree-granting colleges and universities, five community colleges and five theological schools. But numbers are numbers. What distinguishes Kansas City colleges is quality.

Rockhurst College is generally regarded as one of the nation's leading universities. Park College in Parkville, Missouri, and Avila College are both highly respected private colleges. The Fine Arts Series of William Jewell College in Liberty, Missouri, provides world-renowned music and cultural events in its annual concert series.

The Universiy of Missouri at Kansas City boasts one of the top dental schools in the country, a fine law school, and an outstanding theater department. Two major medical schools are part of the area's educational community with new doctors training at UMKC and the University of Kansas Medical Center and College of Health Sciences.

The Linda Hall Library of Science and Technology ranks second only to Harvard University in amount of reference materials, housing more than 500,000 volumes and 13,000 current scientific journals in thirty-five languages.

Kansas City also is a research center. Midwest Research Institute is based here and conducts detailed studies for industry, government and other groups.

Who in Europe, or in America for that matter, knows that Kansas City is one of the loveliest cities on earth? And yet it is true. The downtown section is like any other in the United States, with its violent contrasts of skyscraper and wasteland. But the residential section is a masterpiece of city planning. The streets follow the curves of the hills or the winding of streams. Flowering shrubs encircle the houses. The homes themselves, designed in the best of taste, are artfully grouped in an immense park whose trees are unequaled in variety and luxuriance. At street crossings an antique statue, three shafts of Grecian columns rise from a carpet of low-growing foliage. Few cities have been built with so much regard for beauty.

Andre Maurois

109

Kansas City is still a populist city; one that would have teased the blood of Sherwood Anderson, the psalmodic novelist of Midwestern America, who wrote a book called **Hello Towns**. *People will greet you, address you "Sir," and this is as true of the well-to-do who live near Cliff Drive in the country-club district [sic] as of the humble and tattered whose huts are northeast or near the East or West Bottoms. Courtesy is the strength of a nation, and rudeness, according to the ancient historian of Rome, Livy, is the symptom of the decline of an empire.*

Edward Dahlberg

111

For better or worse, cities are often known by their athletic teams, sports facilities, and superstars. So, in the fifties and early sixties when the Kansas City Athletics were the laughingstock of baseball, Kansas City was labeled a bush-league town. Things changed forever in 1963 when the Kansas City Chiefs appeared on the scene. They won the Super Bowl in 1970 and the area has been a classy major league stop ever since.

Baseball. With local ownership in the hands of Ewing Kauffman, the Royals are perennial pennant contenders and play-off participants. Royals Stadium, the site of the 1973 All-Star game, is generally considered the best in baseball.

Football. The proud Chiefs have a championship past and one of the most spirited – and classiest – organizations in the NFL. Plush Arrowhead Stadium, seating 78,000 and adjacent to Royals Stadium, is ideal in every detail.

Basketball. The 1978-79 division champs, The Kansas City Kings, are counting on Phil Ford, Otis Birdsong, Scott Wedman, and cast to keep them on top. The team's local ownership warrants top support while column-free Kemper Arena is the team's home court.

Kansas City is also a mecca of sorts for college sports, with both Missouri and Kansas universities so close to the city. The National Association of Intercollegiate Athletics (NAIA) basketball tournament is a national classic. For six days each spring thirty-two teams from rural America knock heads until only one is king of the NAIA mountain. The schools are small, but the talent is big, with many NAIA graduates being NBA stars.

Kansas City's top superstar has no uniform and no home field. He is Tom Watson, Golfer of the Year, year after year. His style and success characterize the city's emergence as the Sports Capital of Mid-America.

113

Starlight Theater, Lyric Theater, Missouri
Repertory Theatre, an outstanding
Philharmonic orchestra, the Kansas City
Ballet, and an active Performing Arts
Foundation make Kansas City a cultural
hub.

Starlight, one of the most successful
outdoor theaters in the United States, each
summer features top Broadway and
Hollywood productions.

Not to be outdone in the fall, Lyric Theater
showcases the finest in opera – from Tosca to
Of Mice and Men.

The nationally acclaimed Missouri
Repertory Theatre spotlights the talents of
world-famous artists and directors and
annually offers the best in stage classics in the
spectacular Helen Spencer Center for the
Performing Arts on the campus of the
University of Missouri-Kansas City.

The Kansas City Philharmonic excites
audiences with the thrill of experiencing
music the moment it happens. Performances
range from classical works to the Saturday
Night Pops series of today's sounds. Special
festivals such as the nationally applauded
Leonard Bernstein Festival celebrate the
accomplishments of individual talents. The
Philharmonic also takes music to children
with more than a score of Lollipop and Young
Persons concerts in area schools and
theaters.

An even wider variety of the performing
arts enter the classrooms of Kansas City each
year with the city's Young Audiences
organization. Through Young Audiences,
small ensembles of professional artists
perform music, dance, and theater in schools
throughout the metropolitan area.

In the world of dance, the Kansas City
Ballet gives the city the distinction of being
host to the state's only professional resident
dance company. These talented performers
blend the grace of classical ballet with
contemporary choreography in a six-month
season each year. Similarly, Mimewock
teams the language of dance with the gentle,
expressive art of mime.

To help showcase the arts in Kansas City,
the Performing Arts Foundation has saved
the historic Folly Theater, restoring the
turn-of-the-century playhouse to its original
grandeur.

Nowhere is the interest in keeping fit more evident than in Kansas City. City parks are laced with jogging trails, and marathons, such as the growing Hospital Hill run which draws more than 5,000 runners each year, are just a hint of the city's drive to be active.

Golf is a perennial favorite. Golfers enthusiastically attack par over various public and private courses while young golfers practice with hopes of matching the performance of Kansas City's pro, Tom Watson.

Tennis anyone? With more than 100 conveniently located courts, Kansas City affords ample opportunity for a set-to. Nighttime tennis is particularly popular. Both amateurs and longtime aficionados love to play late into summer evenings with the twinkling lights of the Country Club Plaza as a backdrop. To supplement big court activity, racquetball has been initiated as the newest member of the sports fraternity.

From April to November, the talk around Kansas City's many lakes is spiced with the jargon of the sea. It may surprise some that landlocked Kansas City has sent finalists to national sailboat championships. These crews trained at the weekly regattas here. In addition to the day-sailors, local lakes are home to power-boat enthusiasts and avid water-skiers.

Just as surprising is the spirited presence of the Kansas City Ski Club, largest of the flatland ski groups. After the snow melts, the club keeps busy organizing float trips and other outings through the Ozarks. For the less adventurous, the Kansas City Bike Club couples the thrill of downhill speed with the exercise reality of the uphill climb.

With so much water around, fishing is bound to be great. Rivers and streams boast catfish, bass, crappie and some angling methods Izaac Walton never dreamed of. In addition to traditional finesse with fly rod and spinning reel, some locals add the ancient and venerable art of "noodling." Noodlers attempt to corner a catfish and tickle him to sleep. You have to see it to believe it!

116

From Lewis and Clark to Harry Truman, the Kansas City area boasts of a colorful past, and it is on display for all to see – minutes from downtown Kansas City.

At old Sibley, Missouri, is Fort Osage (far left). Founded in 1808 by William Clark, the fort was the first outpost of the United States in the Louisiana Purchase territory.

Kansas offers the Grinter Place Museum (top left), the first house built in Wyandotte County, and the Shawnee Indian Mission, once a manual training school for Indians and twice territorial capitol of Kansas.

The Harry S. Truman presidential library in Independence (left center) is by far the area's top historical attraction. The library houses papers, books, and mementoes of the late president.

Jesse James still lives in Liberty, Missouri – at least in spirit. A museum marks the spot where Jesse and his brother Frank robbed $66,000 from the Clay County Savings Association – the first daylight bank robbery west of the Mississippi. In neighboring Kearney, Missouri, is the James Farm Home Museum (bottom left) and the cemetery where Jesse is buried.

At Lake Jacomo is Missouri Town – a settlement built in 1855 and later restored to preserve a way of life that is rapidly vanishing.

119

Kansas City is at the heart of an area steeped in Mid-Americana. Just east of here is the stately country town of Lexington, site of the bloodiest victories of Confederate General Sterling Price. In today's more tranquil times, the battlefield blossoms with the gold of wild mustard, a local delicacy.

Equally beautiful is the quaint valley town of Weston (middle center), whose narrow streets are fronted with porticoed, classic, revival homes. Weston is one of the largest tobacco markets in the West. Antique curing sheds are commonplace, and every fall the percussive patter of the tobacco auctioneer draws buyers, sellers, and spectators. This is literally a town time left behind. In the midst of its booming mid-century river trade, the Missouri up and wandered off, abandoning the town several miles inland. Now Weston is best known for the McCormick distillery, open to the public and celebrating over a hundred years of fine bourbon making.

North past Weston is St. Joseph, Missouri (top center), home of the pony express. You can still see the stables from which "Little Johnnie" Frey galloped westward to establish a mail route that would "save California for the Union." Buffalo Bill, "Pony" Bob Haslem, and outlaws Jack Slade and Jesse James rode out of St. Joe, some to fame, some to infamy.

Thirty miles outside of Kansas City is frontier Ft. Leavenworth (bottom center), with its museum of horse-drawn vehicles. And farther west is Abilene, destination of the big Texas cattle drives. Here on the prairie stands the spare frame house of favorite son Dwight Eisenhower, always a tourist mecca along with the presidential library and museum.

The national Agricultural Hall of Fame is in Bonner Springs, Kansas. From there it's a short jaunt to the lovely Flint Hills (far right), lush with a thick, cattle-fattening cover of bluestem grasses. William Allen White called the Flint Hills grass "the most important crop in the kingdom of the big red steer."

BATTLE of LEXINGTON SEPT. 18·19·20 1861

The Ozarks aren't as lofty as the Smokies nor as majestic as the Rockies, but for country charm they have no equal. Clear, blue streams and lush, green forests blend with narrow, winding valleys and steep, rocky ridges to create an unspoiled beauty that lures outdoorsmen like artist Thomas Hart Benton. In Travel & Leisure, Benton described the delights of an Ozark float trip: "I do not know of anything comparable to the charm of gliding down an Ozark stream....

"The Ozarks are heavily wooded. From the top of any ridge you look over vast stretches of timber....the country is not a true wilderness....Nevertheless, when you float the streams the impression is that of a wilderness. Most of the banks are high with the close-knit foliage of overhanging trees on one side and out-jutting limestone bluffs on the other. Ancient gray trunks from long-fallen forest monarchs, thrust downwards into the water....Grapevines, as thick as a man's leg, twist upward into the tree tops or hang out over the water. Willow trees and young sycamores often form tight thickets along the bars....

"Birds abound: eagles, hawks, herons, turkeys, buzzards, ducks – down to the smallest twitterers. Beavers and musk-rats now live their aquatic lives relatively undisturbed, and often the little gray fox ...will watch you slither down a riffle. On rare occasions you catch the golden flash of the wily bobcat, and at night the howl of the timber wolf may penetrate your dreams....

"When's the best time to go to Ozark-land? It's in the spring, of course, when the redbud trees bloom and the azalea and dogwood blossoms shine, starlike, through the translucent green of the awakening forest – and when there's plenty of water, upstream as well as down. But all times are good."

The
Next American
Experience

Searching, suffering, working, winning: the great cycle of the American Experience, plot of countless novels, the same glorious epic flickering Saturday after Saturday on movie screens across the land.

To this day it's primarily a story of transience. We alone among the world's major powers have settled and grown in a place other than where we were born. Stirred by dreams, beckoned by promises, we sailed the Atlantic westward to this vast continent in search of what we were to become. The magnitude of that destiny drove us farther: southward to Virginia, the Carolinas, Georgia; then westward along a north and south front stretching the length of this land, westward across the Appalachians to the rich, rolling midsection, to the Mississippi Valley; then westward across Missouri to the great plains, up and over the Rockies, down to the golden sands of our westernmost shore. Searching, suffering, working, winning — countless hardships, countless battles, countless triumphs; but for a restless, transient people, always countless more.

America's story is the composite of that of its people and its cities. For a brief time in the mid-1800s, microcosm and macrocosm touched: Kansas City was the far western edge of America's consciousness, the fleeting promise of the American Dream. But the country pushed onward as she always had, pushed ever westward in pursuit of a still greater grasp on that age-old promise.

Finally land ran out. We chased north to Alaska; then westward across another ocean to Hawaii. After that, there was nowhere else to go, no more open spaces. Whatever we were searching for had to be found in what we already had, what we already were.

Today Kansas City and other midwestern cities watch as America's search inevitably turns inward. Four hundred years of history documents an undeniable pattern of movement from east to west, from rural community to coastal megalopolis. Logic tells us the trend must change. Ecology has been but one of the issues contributing to the unpopularity of the megalopolis; and from a business standpoint, higher costs and a faster pace make centrality increasingly attractive.

Which means, in Kansas City's interpretation, that America is coming home to the heartland — searching, perhaps, for something she failed to find her first time through. For Kansas City this is at once the chance and the challenge: the chance to be vindicated, appreciated; and yet the challenge to maintain control, to avoid becoming overwhelmed.

Those contemporary products of the Kansas City Spirit feel that they're ready to handle both the benefits and the problems of being an inland capital. The lessons of men like William Rockhill Nelson and J. C. Nichols have sunk in deeply here, and it's been a long time since city fathers have sat back complacently on their Kansas City steaks. Today they speak earnestly of their "legacy of leadership" and of the need to do more things — and do them right.

And so they preach economic rather than industrial development. They combat inner-city decay with mammoth redevelopment projects. They build a futuristic airport that they won't grow into for another twenty years and may not grow out of for generations. They build new hospitals and a half-dozen community colleges at a clip. They even construct their second AMA-accredited medical school and develop a teaching method unknown anywhere else in the country. At the time of the Bicentennial, they create a $5.3 billion building boom with what they proudly boast is seventy-five percent private money.

Yet this is brick and mortar with a soul. A group of citizens continuously raises money from the business community to build and maintain a fountain a year. And always in its construction and restoration programs, Kansas City's emphasis is on people. Rarely has so much been done for beauty's sake alone as is traditionally done commercially in Kansas City. Benches and trees, sculpture and fountains, patios and plazas — none necessary to carry out the city's commerce — but a joyous humane affirmation of the ancient purpose of the city: to bring people together.

The prairie isn't empty any longer. Its hum comes from more than the rustle of trees, its glow from more than the glint of sunlight on desolate limestone cliffs.

Out here there's been ample time to think, to plan — and Kansas City has developed a deep-seated determination to preserve the Kansas City Experience as something decidedly worth the search.

Today many Kansas Citians fully expect *Kansas City* to be the next, and possibly the greatest, American Experience. Why not? America's westward trek has never been primarily a directional thing. In this country's historical context, west stands for all that America — all that man — hopes to find, to enjoy: personal opportunity, economic potential, comfort, contentment, family security. In the year 1857 Robert Van Horn stood before a group of rustic but hopeful people who had staked their future on the success of that muddy plot that was then Kansas City. "The West is found!" boomed Van Horn, and the Kansas City audience cheered their wholehearted approval. They still do.